Great Texas

Don't miss these other Roadrunner Guides:

Texas Water Recreation
Texas Zoos and Animal Parks
Texas Flea Markets

Great Texas Getaways

A Roadrunner Guide

Ann Ruff

Taylor Publishing Company
Dallas, Texas

Published by Taylor Publishing Company
              1550 West Mockingbird Lane
              Dallas, Texas 75235

Designed by Deborah J. Jackson-Jones

Library of Congress Cataloging-in-Publication Data

Ruff, Ann, 1930–
    Great Texas getaways / Ann Ruff.
        p.   cm. — (A Roadrunner guide)
    Includes index.
    ISBN 0-87833-657-5 : $10.95
    1. Resorts—Texas—Guidebooks. 2. Texas—Description
and travel—1981– —Guidebooks. I. Title. II. Series.
TX907.3.T4R82   1992
647.9476401—dc20   91-46566
                                                   CIP

Printed in the United States of America

10 9 8 7 6 5 4 3 2

*To Richard Wright for making these great getaways
even greater getaways.*

CONTENTS

KEY TO SYMBOLS
AND PRICES

SYMBOLS

 Children Welcome

 Pets Welcome

 RV Accommodations Available

PRICES

$ Budget: Under $60

$$ Moderate: $60 to $100

$$$ Exclusive: Over $100

$$$$ Very Exclusive: Over $1000

Trips Down Texas Roads Less Traveled

Some people collect souvenirs, some collect great art, and some collect money. I prefer collecting memories. And the most enduring memories are of places and people. Nothing is as satisfying as spending time in an idyllic setting relaxing and doing things you enjoy, and it's even better if you have someone to share the memory with.

Texas is blessed with a plethora of these special places for relaxation, fun, and adventure. Most are easy drives from the major cities, but a few are out on the lone prairie. Others are *way* out on the lone prairie. Yet, these are perhaps the best of all getaways and well worth the getting there.

Just because many of these great getaways allow children, this doesn't detract from their romantic ambiance. Some of the best weekends we have had were at dude ranches such as the Mayan and big resorts such as Chain-O-Lakes and Port Royal. We did go as often as possible in the off-season because the pace is slower, the weather nicer, and sometimes the rates are lower. And for couples who want some time to themselves, off-season has even more advantages.

Great getaways come in all sorts of adventures. Maybe it's a challenging golf course, a weekend of tennis lessons, a thrilling raft trip down the Rio Grande, or a romantic

carriage ride through the Big Thicket at Chain-O-Lakes. For some, a great getaway is just sitting in the swing at the Guadalupe River Ranch holding hands and watching the sunset.

You will find great getaways for everybody in this book, and if you asked which were my favorites I'd just reply, "I collected wonderful memories at all of them."

When You Want to Get Away from It All
Resorts, Ranches, and Lodges

For travelers in search of relaxation and recreation—whether a rustic retreat or an exciting resort—there's something in Texas for everyone.

Most of these accommodations offer a wide variety of activities. So if you've always wanted to take dance lessons, learn to play tennis, or canoe down a lazy, winding river, you're in luck! Just want to relax with a good book or pitch horseshoes with new friends? Or maybe you want to spend your time doing all the activities you always dreamed of trying someday. If the Texas coast beckons you, there's also special oceanside attractions waiting to welcome you. Whatever takes your fancy—it's all here in this collection of the most irresistible retreats in Texas.

IDLEWILDE LODGE

Rt. 2, Box 326
Comfort 78013
800-992-3844
512-995-3844

Hosts: Connie and Hank Engle

Accommodations: 9 bedrooms, 2 cabins.

Rates: $$ (full breakfast included)

Location: Take second Comfort exit off I-10 West. Go left on FM 523 to blinking light. Go left on FM 473 1.3 miles. Go through gate on the right opposite Idlewilde mailbox. Close gate and go through another gate. Idlewilde is just past the second gate.

Amenities: Small swimming pool, 2 lighted tennis courts, outdoor pavilion with barbecue pit, bath house, kennels, van service to San Antonio airport and Sea World, playground, horseback rides, hiking, birdwatching, ideal for small meetings or weddings and reunions.

Restrictions: Smoking outside only. Three-day cancellation notice required for deposit refund.

Connie and Hank Engle really put it on the line with, "We offer you an unconditional guarantee that you will enjoy your stay at Idlewilde." How can you beat a deal like that? And people have been enjoying their stay at Idlewilde for a long, long time. The Texas Historical Medallion explains that Idlewilde, came into existence as a girls' camp in 1905. Known as "Haven in the Hills," girls came to Idlewilde for more than 60 years to sing camp songs, play camp games, make lasting friendships, and learn to love the Texas Hill Country. You can go back those 60 years and do all those campy things, but in nice modern accommodations.

The Lodge or Main House has 3 bedrooms and 2 baths. Meals are served in the comfortable dining room, and Connie goes all out with a big country breakfast. The only television set is in the living room area of the Lodge, which is furnished with antiques from an eclectic blend of eras. A gigantic fireplace offers a cozy retreat on those brisk Hill Country wintry days. During the summer, a constant breeze blows through the Lodge's many windows, and even though it is air conditioned, Mother Nature rarely needs any help.

The Western House has 3 bedrooms and 1 bath, a kitchen, living room, and porch. Newly renovated, this home gives the feel of true country charm. The Variety House has the same accommodations, and its unique name comes from the fun decor. One bedroom has a sports theme, another is a railroad buff's dream, and the third, with a plethora of stuffed animals to hug and cuddle, is for animal lovers.

The Lighthouse Cabin is a studio-size accommodation with a bedroom, a bath, a kitchenette, and a wonderful porch for wildlife watching. The Artist Cabin is a studio-size house. The working canvas and finished artwork you'll find inside will urge you to be creative. However, sitting on its porch and just enjoying the woods is too enticing, so don't expect to accomplish much except regaining a real peace of mind.

"Customized Service" is the motto at Idlewilde. No hours are set for you to check in or out. Breakfast can be in your room, on the porch, on the lawn, at the pool, or even in bed. Whatever you want to do, whenever you want to do it, is just fine at Idlewilde.

Pets are welcome, which is definitely a different touch. Just keep Bowser on his leash or in the kennels when he's not in the house with you. Pokey, the family dog, and the melange of cats are all friendly types, so Bowser will have a good vacation too.

The pool is hardly an Olympic training area but does offer a cool dip. However, don't forget about the Guadalupe River that's just a short walk through the woods. Also, the horses are all easygoing and will take you for a slow ride down the trails.

And just in case you don't know about Comfort, you've missed one of the best small (and we do mean small) towns in Texas. Comfort boasts the only monument to the Union in the entire South. In 1862, a group of German Unionists were on their way to Mexico to avoid fighting for slavery. They were ambushed by the Confederates in the Nueces River Massacre, and after the Civil War their bones were buried under the "Treue Der Union" Monument.

Today, Comfort is basking in tourism with its plethora of antique shops, its flea market, an armadillo farm where the Apelt family makes armadillo shell baskets, and an old railroad tunnel. (Yes, there really is a railroad tunnel in Texas, but it's the only one.) It is now home to millions of bats. During the summer, the bat show is a Hill Country answer to a big city laser show.

So, now you see why the Engels can unconditionally guarantee that you will enjoy your stay at Idlewilde.

VICTORIA PALMS RESORT

602 North Victoria Road
Donna 78537
512-464-7801

Accommodations: Motel rooms, motel suites, mobile homes, RV spaces.

Rates: $$

Location: Off Expressway 83 between Harlingen and McAllen.

Amenities: Swimming pool, 2 therapy pools, exercise room, ceramic shop, workshop, arts and crafts space, Ping-Pong, card rooms, billiards, library, shuffleboard, horseshoes, outdoor grills, planned activities, arranged tours, dance lessons, post office, laundry rooms, restaurant, barber and beauty shops, car wash, 24-hour security, summer rates, conference rooms, golf and tennis arrangements, fishing and hunting arrangements, storage area for extra vehicles, maid service.

Restrictions: Written notification for full deposit refund before Sept. 1; no deposit refund after Nov. 1. Pets allowed only at discretion of management. Extra charge for guests. This is an ADULTS ONLY park. Children may only visit, and all guests must be registered with the management.

You can stay so busy taking classes at Victoria Palms, you'll forget that it's a resort for play and relaxation. During the week you start with an exercise class, then a square dance class, then a round dance class, then an oil painting class, break for bowling lessons, throw some horseshoes, and play shuffleboard. Then, it's back for ballroom dancing and advanced square dancing. At the end of a day full of activities like these, you will be more than ready for one of the therapy pools.

Living really is easy down in Texas' Magic Valley. RV owners find this part of the Lone Star State the perfect spot to spend a few days, a few weeks, a few months, or maybe forever. Trips to Mexico for bargains are a walk across the bridge. Padre Island's sparkling beaches and superb seafood are only a few miles down the expressway, and yet there's plenty to see in the Magic Valley. Zoo lovers can't get to **Brownsville's Gladys Porter Zoo** enough times. There's good food and hospitality at the historic **San Juan Hotel** in San Juan, and the magnificent **La Borde House** in Rio Grande City is worth the short drive just to see the gorgeous antiques. History buffs can relive the Mexican War, read numerous historical markers all through the area, and ride the country's last hand-pulled ferry across the Rio Grande.

Yet you never have to leave Victoria Palms, except for maybe a trip to the supermarket. You don't even really need the supermarket because the restaurant serves up great buffets. You can have lunch, get your hair done, shop at the gift shop, go dancing, and never move more than a few steps. This little town/resort has it all.

The modern, spacious motel suites are fully furnished, and the kitchen is equipped with pots, pans, and table service for four. You have a phone and television, and all you need to bring is your toothbrush and a change of clothes. Well, maybe your square dance costume would be nice to have, too.

If you are dragging along a boat or a car behind your RV, there's a full-security storage area to park it in. Then, it's time to go sign up for some of those dance classes. After church on Sunday, it's tea dancing time followed by an ice cream social. Many special events are on the agenda, and you have plenty of opportunities to meet new friends and visit with old ones. Many Victoria Palms guests return year after year.

So, head for the Magic Valley with its sunny days, friendly people, and the warm hospitality of Victoria Palms Resort.

MO-RANCH

Hunt 78024
512-238-4455

Accommodations: Motel-style rooms, 8 rooms in the Manor House, 3 dormitories, 3 lodges, apartments, campground, RV hookups, retreat facility; total accommodations are 500.

Rates: $$

Location: Take FM 1340 west out of Hunt.

Amenities: Cafeteria, swimming pool, river sports including a 30-foot river slide, hiking, 3 tennis courts, horseshoes, shuffleboard, team sports, table games, fenced playground, conference facilities, gift shop, library, snack shop, laundry facilities, canoe rentals, church services.

Restrictions: No pets whatsoever, no smoking in any areas whatsoever, alcohol only in private quarters, no loud noises, dress in keeping with a Christian environment, to swim in the river you must pass a swimming test in the pool, pay phones only, deposit refund if cancellation is in writing 2 months prior to arrival.

Even though the historic Mo-Ranch can easily accommodate up to 500 guests at one time, it is so beautiful that it is still a great getaway. Dan Moran began his unique ranch back in 1936 when no one but the Civilian Conservation Corps was doing construction. But Dan Moran was president of the great Continental Oil Company, and the oil business was booming. When he bought the ranch, the 1929 ranch house, with its native limestone, red tile roof, and unusual stairwells and passages, had already been built, but Moran began a 11-year project to make his newly christened Mo-Ranch the way he wanted it.

Moran must have loved winter in the Hill Country because the fireplaces can hold massive oak, cedar, and mesquite logs. The guest lodge fireplace displays cave rocks and rough cut gemstones like quartzite, geodes, amethyst, and agate interspersed with petrified wood.

Summer must have had its appeal, too. In 1938, Moran added a huge swimming pool which has "Mo-Ranch" spelled in tiny colored squares of tile across the front.

Moran had an unlimited supply of oil-field pipe, so many of the great columns in the buildings are not giant cedar trees, as they appear. They are made of pipe that has been tempered, curved, and then painted to simulate natural wood, complete with knotholes. To span a gorge and provide access to a dormitory, Moran built a 290-foot footbridge out of this durable pipe.

Even a chapel for the private worship of the Moran family was incorporated into the sprawling 6,800-acre retreat. It also remains in harmony with the surrounding hills, trees, rocks, and pristine Guadalupe River.

The Moran family were Catholics, but in 1929 Mo-Ranch was purchased by the Presbyterian Synod. In 1950, the State of Texas bought 6,500 acres for the Kerr Wildlife Management Area, and today the church owns 377 acres and the permanent buildings.

All denominations are welcome to book Mo-Ranch's facilities; it is a very popular retreat for many small and large groups. When church groups are not using the ranch, other groups are invited to hold meetings. But, for individuals looking for a getaway, Mo-Ranch is available when not fully booked with groups. The staff at this lovely site wants everyone to enjoy the beauty that has been lavished on the Texas Hill Country, particularly at Mo-Ranch.

Pheasant Run has motel-like rooms with private baths, 2 double beds, and air conditioning. The Manor House also has 8 rooms that can be rented individually. Apartments are rather modestly furnished, but have complete kitchen facilities. The newest accommodations at Mo-Ranch are Flato and Wynne Lodges. Rooms have 2 double beds and private baths.

The King Dining Hall provides 3 delicious meals daily in air-conditioned comfort with a magnificent view and very reasonable prices. Meal reservations must be made a week in advance.

The best time of year for Mo-Ranch is September through May. The weather is brisk, group usage is much lower, and the Hill Country is gorgeous with its autumn colors. Fall is the best time for bird watching too. Yet don't forget spring with its fields of blue bonnets, art shows, and festivals. Pheasant Run, Flato, and Wynne Lodges offer rooms during this season.

Texas owes Dan Moran a real thank-you for leaving behind this very special place. Once you go there, you will never forget Mo-Ranch.

CAMP WARNECKE RESORTS

317 West Lincoln
New Braunfels 78130
512-620-3500

Accommodations: 1-, 2-, and 3-bedroom luxury condominiums.

Rates: $$ (seasonal rates)

Location: Take I-35 to New Braunfels. Take Exit 187 and go west toward downtown on Seguin Ave. Turn right on Garden Street and cross Comal River Bridge. Take first left turn after the bridge to rental office.

Amenities: Swimming pool, hot tub, clubhouse, picnic area, tubes furnished.

Restrictions: No pets, adult registration only, 2-night minimum stay, 3-night minimum stay holiday weekends, 2-week cancellation notice required for refund.

No matter what time of year you come to enjoy the flavor of New Braunfels, one of the ideal escapes is Camp Warnecke Resorts. The modern condominiums are built of native wood and stone and blend gracefully with the natural beauty of the setting. You are only a few short blocks from downtown, but it seems as if you are far from any form of city life.

Perched right on the Comal, Texas' shortest river, you can grab your tube and jump right in for a relaxing float. There's easy access at several places along the bank when you're ready to repeat the tubing jaunt. The cold spring water may be a bit too frigid in the winter, but then you have those super hot tubs for a relaxing end to a fun-filled day.

The condominiums have it all: microwaves, washer/dryer,

color television with cable, and telephones. Each unit also has a covered parking spot. You will find standard condominium decor and modern furnishings, but you do have the choice of a unit with a fireplace, which is not a bad idea in the winter.

Everyone who has ever been to New Braunfels loves it. The over-fifty crowd remembers when the town was on the sleepy side and resorts were limited to old Camp Warnecke and The Other Place. Both were on the ratty side, but back in those days, nobody knew about hot tubs. Even the motels were not the well-known chains. (Does anyone remember the 747 Motel?)

Those days are long gone, and absolutely no one regrets their passing. The Other Place is still there, but it, too, has been converted into condominiums. During the summer season, it is hard to find lodging anywhere in this popular town, and reservations are a necessity. If at all possible, try to schedule your getaway time in May or September. The only disadvantage of a late summer or fall visit is that the rivers (Guadalupe and Comal) tend to run very slowly if the summer has been dry.

Just up the street from Camp Warnecke Resorts is the fabulous water park, the **Schlitterbahn**. Golfers can walk to the public course a few blocks away. Camp Warnecke is one of the most popular resorts in New Braunfels, probably because you can just about forget your car.

But, before you put away the car keys, browse around the **Factory Outlet Mall** on I-35 and visit the **Natural Bridge Caverns** and **Wildlife Park**. And don't forget **Gruene**, which is famous for the oldest dance hall in Texas; they sho nuff still two-step here every weekend. A jillion antique shops are in the area, and if the Comal River is too short for you, go on out River Road and ride the rapids on the

Guadalupe. Here you have it all—a luxurious resort, New Braunfels' Comal River, and the convenience of good restaurants just off the square. Remember, a meal at **Wolfgang's Keller** at the **Prince Solms Inn** on San Antonio Street is a "must."

TERLINGUA RANCH

Terlingua Route, Box 220
Alpine 79830
915-371-2416

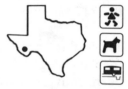

Accommodations: 32 air-conditioned motel rooms.

Rates: $ (special group rates available)

Location: Take State Highway 118 from Alpine south for 62 miles, then drive 17 miles off the main highway. (As the old-timers used to say, "You go south from Fort Davis until you come to the place where the rainbows wait for rain, and the big river is kept in a stone box, and water runs up hill, and the mountains float in the air, except at night when they go away to play with other mountains.")

Amenities: Campgrounds, RV hookups, dining room, swimming pool, riding stables, auto gas, gift shop, airport (4800-foot graded gravel surface).

Indian legends record that the Great Creator had a pile of rubble left over when he finished shaping the heavens and the earth. He threw the rubble into a heap and formed the Big Bend Country. Writers, artists, and lovers of the great outdoors continue to extol the beauty and wonder of the Great Creator's rubble, but no matter how many books are written, photographs taken, or pictures painted, Big Bend's majesty is never exhausted.

Terlingua Ranch is a wonderful place to make your headquarters as you explore this majestic park. When you visit here, you will soon become aware of the vastness, the spectacular landscapes of rugged mountains and wide open spaces. The air is so clean, so clear, that some say you can see all the way into the day after tomorrow.

Your basic motel room is not a fancy lodge, but you certainly won't lack for scenery. And Terlingua Ranch has 1,100 miles of roads to enjoy the majesty of the area. And hikers would have to spend a lifetime to explore the beauty of Big Bend. But, one of the best ways to experience all this rough outdoors is on a trail ride with a guide. Kids under 12 stay back at the ranch for free pony rides.

Hayrides and cookouts are part of the special activities offered, as well as overnight trail rides and campouts. During the spring and summer, outdoor barbecues and country-western dances are part of the agenda. You are always welcome to use the outdoor grills by the motel.

About 100 million years ago this area was an ocean, but as nature took her course this heart of the Chihuahua Desert became a geological showplace. Here the spectator is overwhelmed with what nature can do when she has the time. No wonder adventurers return over and over again, never tiring of Big Bend's wonders.

LAGUNA DIABLO RESORT

P.O. Box 420608
Del Rio 78842
512-774-2422

Hosts: Jim and Betty Sanders

Accommodations: 10 apartments, 6 with 2 bedrooms, 4 with 1 bedroom.

Rates: $$

Location: On the Devils River arm of Lake Amistad. Take Highway 277–377 north of Del Rio, turn on RR 2. Go 6 miles, turn right through rock archway. Stay to your right and go 2.2 miles. Turn left at "Laguna Diablo" sign with large arrow.

Amenities: Each apartment is completely furnished with washer/dryer, linens, towels, flatware, cookware, and dishes. Cold drink machine, ice, and pay phone available.

Restrictions: No pets, 2-night minimum stay, no restaurant, no grocery store, boat launching 4 miles from resort.

Lake Amistad is truly an anachronism in this arid Chihuahuan Desert. With nary a tree for a jillion miles, suddenly you come upon a vast lake with water the color of brilliant azure. Sparkling Lake Amistad is the successful result of a joint project between Mexico and the United States and is the third largest international manmade lake in the world.

"Amistad" means "friendship" in Spanish, and this is the key word for the area. The dam is crowned with two impressive monuments, each an eagle, the national emblem of both countries. Boats cruise and enjoy both borders of the lake. The United States' side of Amistad is controlled by the

National Park Service, so boats can only be launched at des-
ignated sites. However, you are free to dock at any spot on
the raw and primitive coastline. The Park Service also provides beaches, marinas, campgrounds, and nature walks.

Up on the Devils River arm of Lake Amistad, about 20 miles
north of Del Rio, you can really get away for that peace and
quiet you're looking for. Jim and Betty Sanders have built 10
comfortable furnished apartments on their property, which
is sort of out in the middle of nowhere. While the decor is
"motel-functional," the setting is wonderful. You overlook a
deep, dark blue ribbon of water that is the Devils River
before it becomes Lake Amistad. The grounds are filled
with unique bird houses resembling Spanish castles. A cat
may wander by to check you out, and you may see a couple
of silly goats because Betty runs sort of an adoption agency
for lost and strayed billies and nannies.

Mitch, with his strange yellow goat eyes, is a sweetie, but
he loves attention. He won't exactly butt you, but he is very
pushy. Gus is black with a twitchy brown tail, and he and
Mitch are great buddies.

Life at Laguna Diablo is totally serene. You'll hear an occasional boat in the distance, birds twittering, and perhaps a
ba-a-a-a from the goats. No video games bleep, no televisions blare, and no kids scream from a pool. You have to
make your own entertainment. How about that book you've
been meaning to read? And instead of watching television,
try gazing at the bright stars and gorgeous moon shimmering on the water.

The closest boat launch is 4 miles away at Rough Canyon
Marina, which also carries fishing supplies and gas. But,
there is no restaurant or grocery store in the area, so stock
up with food. Of course, fishermen love the lake with its
"big ones," and even though they can't launch at Laguna
Diablo, they can pull their boat onto shore.

Del Rio has plenty of fun, and it's one of the most popular border towns. Don't miss wine tasting at the 100-year-old **Val Verde Winery**. Then be sure to drive by the **Brinkly Mansion**. "Dr." Brinkly made millions during the Depression selling goat gland transplants to old men to make them "frisky" again. On the grounds of the quaint **Whitehead Museum** is the tomb of a famous old reprobate in Texas, Judge Roy Bean. His historic saloon, dubbed **Law West of the Pecos**, is a few miles west at Langtry and you should definitely visit it too. The one near his grave is merely a replica.

Across the border is **Ciudad Acuna**, another favorite town. Shops on the main drag offer every souvenir you ever wanted, and down at **Mrs. Crosby's**, a wonderful old Spanish colonial bar, the bartender mixes the best drinks in Mexico. Just watch out for those tequila sours! At **Lando's** you'll find perfect service, a huge menu, and excellent food. Dress is casual and prices are moderate.

In fact, don't miss any of the Del Rio-Lake Amistad area. If you like Indian rock painting, there's **Seminole Canyon**. Now with **High Bridge Adventures**, you can experience rock art on a 3-hour pontoon-boat excursion to two shelters. Call 915-292-4464 for reservations. If you like water sports, you have the beautiful lake; if you want a touch of old Mexico, there's Ciudad Acuna. The sun shines every day, the fish are always biting, and at Laguna Diablo you can count on Mitch to want his head scratched.

STONEWALL VALLEY RANCH

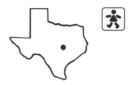

3810 Medical Parkway
Austin 78756
512-454-0476
512-644-2380 (ranch)

Hosts: Don and Velna Jackson

Accommodations: 2-bedroom, 1-bath guesthouse.

Rates: $$

Location: Take 290 to FM 1623 (just east of Stonewall) and go north 3 miles. Then go east 2 miles on FM 2721. Ranch is on the left (the north side of LBJ Ranch).

Amenities: 13 fishing ponds, hiking, jeep tour, children welcome.

Restrictions: Smoking on porch only, no pets.

Don and Velna Jackson are such nice people, and so are their kids, Donna and Donny. But the real star of Stonewall Ranch is Captain Twiggs, a gigantic red and white Longhorn steer. Talk about a ham! (Or should I say steak?) Anyway, Captain Twiggs was born for the camera. This big guy will stand stock still for hours while people hoist themselves on his back, hang cowboy hats on his horns, and make all sorts of silly gestures. Twiggs may get a glazed look in his eyes, but he endures such shenanigans with stoic calmness. Such patience has brought Twiggs much fame (maybe even some fortune as well) and attention. He goes to parades, is invited to parties (including one held in the lobby of Austin's Stouffer Hotel), poses for photographs, lets all sorts of people ride him (including Ann Richards), and contentedly chews his cud throughout any affair. Twiggs' social calendar stays booked.

Captain Twiggs is one of a show herd of Longhorns the

Jacksons raise on their ranch. The family takes their best Longhorns to stock shows where they usually win or place in nearly every event. When Don describes his ranch and his cattle, he talks about them with pride, and rightfully so, because he's only been in the Longhorn business since 1981.

You don't go to Stonewall Valley Ranch just to ride Captain Twiggs though. You can take your fishing pole and try your luck in one of the ponds. If that pond doesn't yield a big one, there are twelve more to try. With 455 acres to roam, you should take your hiking boots, even though Don really enjoys taking guests on a jeep tour of the ranch. You can count on lots of stories as you bounce over rocks and gullies. Kids love Stonewall Ranch because Donna and Donny show them how to find fresh eggs, shovel hay, and feed the livestock.

The Jacksons bought the ranch back in 1974 when it had the remnants of a small house, a shed, and a hay barn. During renovation, they discovered that the hay barn was actually the owner's original homestead. Built in the 1920s, it was a simple, frame ranch house with no plumbing and no electricity. Today it is a charming guesthouse known as The Homestead. The kitchen is decorated in antiques, including a wood-burning stove the Jacksons found in Colorado. But you'll find contemporary kitchenware as well.
The refrigerator is stocked with assorted goodies for breakfast; you fix your own whenever you feel like it. You can bring your own groceries for other meals, but Fredericksburg is just down the road and has many excellent restaurants.

When you aren't posing with Captain Twiggs, tour the **LBJ Ranch**, or explore the **Nimitz World War II Museum** and shops along Fredericksburg's Main Street. The **Oberhellman Vineyard** and the **Grape Valley Vineyard** are also nearby and open for visitors every Saturday.

So ya'll come on down to Stonewall Valley. The Jacksons and Captain Twiggs are always ready for group photos.

JOHN NEWCOMBE'S TENNIS RANCH

P.O. Box 469
New Braunfels 78130
800-262-NEWK
800-292-7080 (Texas)
512-625-9105

Accommodations: 1- and 2-bedroom condominiums and luxury motel rooms and cabin accommodations for groups.

Rates: $$ to $$$

Location: Highway 46, 3 miles west of New Braunfels.

Amenities: Swimming pool, pro shop, Jacuzzi spa, 28 Laykold all-weather covered courts (8 lighted), meals, lounge, junior programs (ages 9–18).

Tennis, everyone? If tennis is your game, then pack your racket and book a stint at one of the most successful tennis programs in the country. You can literally eat, live, and breathe tennis during your entire stay.

Nestled deep in the beautiful Texas Hill Country, Newk's is informal and the pace is relaxed. Your tennis clothes and a bathing suit are all you need. However, lots of evening barbecues are held poolside, so toss in your jeans too.

Laugh *and* win! At Newk's you will not only improve your game, you will have a great time, all the time. As John Newcombe says, "First we stress the basics and how they will improve your game, no matter what your level. Second, your stay will be fun!"

Newk's offers a lot of programs. There's literally something for every type of tennis addict. The most popular program is the Two-Day Tennis Package beginning Friday with dinner and ending at lunch on Sunday. Your training includes three clinics, use of all the ranch facilities and a Saturday night western dance. You will play in a fun doubles tournament and maybe even take home one of those special Newk trophies.

The Five-Day Tennis Package begins at 4:00 P.M. on Sunday and continues until Friday noon. Your first day begins with "Tips on Total Tennis," and then you start a series of progressive on-court rotational drills. You will be able to practice your weaker shots and strengthen those that are less difficult for you. No more than five people are ever assigned to each pro, so each guest gets lots of personal attention and instruction.

After you have perfected your strokes, you'll move on to the Advanced Clinic, where you'll work on developing depth, varying spins, and strategies.

You do have to get off the court once in a while, even if it's just to eat. Feast on good homestyle cooking served in the rustic charm of the main lodge. And, if you and your trusty racket need a rest, music and singing are also scheduled for the end-of-the-day fun.

New Braunfels is a fantastic tourist town, and San Antonio

is just 30 minutes down the interstate. So, if a member of your party just doesn't thrill to a perfect backhand, there's plenty of alternative entertainment nearby. But, less avid players might also consider taking some private lessons. They just might find tennis is their game after all.

Newk's is a tennis player's paradise. If you just want to learn a decent backstroke, or if you are getting ready for Wimbleton, Newk's is the place. As John Newcombe puts it, "Tennis is my life, my love. My motivation now is to impart to others, as a teacher, a love for this great game."

T BAR M

Conference Center and Tennis Ranch
P.O. Box 714
New Braunfels 78130
800-292-5469 (Texas)
512-625-7738

Accommodations: 65 villas, 40 rooms.

Rates: $$

Location: 4 miles west of New Braunfels on Highway 46.

Amenities: 12 outdoor tennis courts, 2 indoor tennis courts, athletic field, gymnasium for basketball and volleyball, 2 outdoor swimming pools, jogging trails, rope course, rappelling tower, near Canyon Lake and Guadalupe River, golf also nearby. Conference facilities for 100, youth camp, tennis packages.

Restrictions: No pets.

T Bar M has enjoyed a long-standing reputation for being the perfect spot for fun and relaxation. As early as 1900 the

New Braunfels Country Club was on this site. Next, a dude ranch filled the area with riding trails, and finally in 1967, the property became the T Bar M (the best of them all).

Modern villas cluster around excellent tennis courts. All you have to do is step out of your door and you're ready to take on a worthy opponent. Each villa has 2 bedrooms, 2 baths, a fully equipped kitchen, a fireplace, and handsome furnishings. Although most of the villas are privately owned, they are included in the hotel rental pool. Accommodations are also available at the Country Inn, which has motel-style rooms. If the Villas are booked, you'll be very comfortable at the Country Inn—at lower rates.

Courts are available on a first come, first serve basis (pardon the pun). And for a small fee you can reserve the indoor courts. Other than the indoor courts, all facilities at T Bar M are free to guests.

While the main emphasis is on tennis at T Bar M, you never have to pick up a racket to have a great time. The water aerobic classes are super, and New Braunfels, with its many attractions, is just over the hill.

Those interested in rock climbing may want to practice their rappelling skills on the tower. All climbers must be accompanied by an instructor. The tower and other specialty sports facilities are located in the youth camp area, which is set off from the main area of T Bar M. You'll surely see it if you decide to jog the shady paths through the woods.

Meals are served in the dining room next to the Sports Center (gymnasium), and the fare is good old Hill Country cooking. Check with the registration desk for meal times. While the dining room is not fancy, it does offer a friendly atmosphere and can easily handle large groups.

T Bar M is one of Texas' best mini-resorts.

ENCINITOS RANCH

P.O. Box 3309
Alice 78333
800-222-3824

Accommodations: Camp house for 18 guests, dormitory style, 2 baths.

Rates: $$

Location: You will receive directions with your confirmed reservation. Many guests are met in Alice and escorted to the ranch.

Amenities: Horses, saddles, chaps, bandannas, bedrolls provided.

Restrictions: All children must be accompanied by a parent, no provision for special diets, no pets allowed, no firearms allowed.

Have you ever yearned to go back a hundred years and live the rough and tough life on the range herding cattle and being a cowboy (or cowgirl)? Now you, too, can be a cow-poke on Encinitos Ranch, down in the scrub brush country of South Texas. Encinitos, which means "the little oaks," is 45,000 acres of cattle, horses, oil, and Texas—all found light years away from civilization. But this is no dude ranch. You come here to learn and work. Encinitos offers the satisfaction and thrill of spinning a rope and learning about horses and handling a shooting iron. Report to the camp in jeans, boots, hat, and a long-sleeved shirt. Tenderfoots better bring sun screen, too.

You'll choose your own mount from more than 100 horses in the remuda, and its care will be your responsibility. Your herd may not be Longhorns, but you will be part of the team that drives and brands the cattle and cuts the calves from the herd. Even riding the night herd is expected from cowpokes at Encinitos. However, there are no requirements about singing cowboy ballads to lull the cattle to rest, so don't worry about learning cowboy songs.

After a very hard day on the range, it's a hefty supper around the camp fire near the chuck wagon. Food never tasted as good, even at the finest restaurants, as it does in the open air on the range. After supper, it's a bed roll and a blanket of stars for those weary bones. Just remember, real cowboys did all this and more for only a dollar a day.

A week's schedule will be something like the following:

After your arrival, you'll be given a safety lecture, introduced to your fellow wranglers, and given a bunk in the modern bunkhouse.

On day one, you learn all about your horse and take about a 5-hour ride. Then, it's dinner and bed. You may be assigned fire watch, but that's better than Indian watch.

Day two is devoted to learning about roping calves and handling a six-shooter.

You'll spend the next day rounding up cattle and becoming skilled at riding through that miserable prickly pear cactus and mesquite. The old bed roll will look mighty good after a day of this.

On day four you'll round up strays and participate in another cattle drive. But this time the trail boss takes his wranglers on a night ride with only the moon to light the way.

The dirty work of cutting and branding cattle is scheduled for day five. Remember, that cute little calf weighs 450 pounds.

On the last day you can pretty much do as you please or practice your new skills. Then you'll have to say goodbye to your faithful horse and those hard-working trail hands that led you through six days of riding, roping, and shooting.

If your time is limited and you can't stay the full time, you can sign up for a weekend agenda beginning with lunch on Friday and ending with supper on Monday. Encinitos welcomes cowkids, too.

Food is served in abundance and you'll wolf down every bite. Lots of eggs, bacon, homemade bread, coffee, and potatoes are on the breakfast menu.

Lunch is stew, fried chicken, baked beans, and barbecued ribs.

By dinnertime, you'll be so hungry you won't care what's cooking. Steaks, ribs, fajitas, tacos, and other good chow disappear faster than you can imagine.

Encinitos will send you a detailed list of what to bring, the ranch rules, and other information. You should read it very carefully; you can't just run to the store while riding the range.

At Encinitos guests and wranglers are the only people around for hundreds of square miles, allowing guests to experience a peace and closeness to the earth rarely found in their daily lives. You will leave Encinitos with a real understanding of why men wanted to be cowboys, even at a dollar a day.

INN ON THE RIVER

P.O. Box 1417
209 Barnard Street
Glen Rose 76043
817-897-2101

Host: Peggy Allman

Accommodations: 21 rooms and 3 suites.

Rates: $$ to $$$

Location: Take I-35 W south of Forth Worth to U.S. 67 exit. Go west on 67 about 35 miles.

Amenities: Swimming pool, conference center, gourmet breakfast.

Restrictions: The inn cannot accommodate children or pets. No smoking under any conditions. A nonrefundable deposit of $50 per room per day is required (deposit can be applied to another night or visit should you need to cancel).

Years and years ago it was somewhat fashionable to take a rest cure at a posh sanitarium. The term "sanitarium" has gone out of style, but you can still rest a few days at a fashionable old sanitarium renamed Inn on the River.

In April of 1987 Steve and Peggy Allman purchased the 1919 Snyder Sanitarium, which was little more than a town eyesore. Its original owner, Dr. George P. Snyder, has been described as a clairvoyant, a magnetic healer, a faith healer, and even a self-taught psychiatrist. Whatever "Doctor" Snyder's talents were, the weary and worn sought the good doctor's healing powers for over four decades. The building's prairie architecture is not that unique, but because of Doctor Snyder's colorful contribution to Texas history, the building has been awarded the coveted Texas Historical Landmark medallion.

After a lot of cleaning, scraping, digging, paint, wallpaper, and downright hard work, the Allmans transformed the town relic into an absolutely wonderful country inn. Doctor Snyder never had it so good.

The river that flows by the inn, even though it isn't one of Texas' famous rivers, is very famous among paleontologists. Here in the limestone bed of the Paluxy River are some of the best preserved dinosaur tracks in the Southwest. A wonderful state park protects these birdbath-size tracks so visitors can walk back millions and millions of years in time. Summer is the best time for jumping about in the tracks because the river is low and they are easily visible.

The Paluxy trickles gently by the Inn on the River, but to really appreciate its beauty you'll have to lounge in the old-fashioned wooden-slat lawn chairs that await you on the bank. It's the perfect spot to sit and sip a cool drink. The ancient trees on the lawn are also especially beautiful. The three magnificent, intertwined live oaks are not only included in the inn's logo, but also in a song entitled "The Singing Trees," which was composed long ago by a guest. The song was recorded by an unknown artist named Elvis Presley. The melody did not make Elvis famous, so recordings of it are rare. However, Peggy has a copy and will be delighted to play it for you.

Custom headboards, whether antique, wicker, or brass, are the focal point of every guest room. Each room has its individual wallpaper pattern, and a vintage wardrobe. The baths recall the crisp, all-white rooms with white ceramic wall tiles, plump white faucet handles, and pedestal lavatories.

The huge lobby has been transformed from dark and dismal to light, bright, and charming. A black and white tile floor, grass-papered walls, white beam ceilings, and old-world wicker provide a delightful arena.

This area is nice to visit during any season. If you choose to stay at the inn during the summer, a lovely pool in the large back yard provides the perfect spot to relax. (Although the river is very picturesque, it is not deep enough for swimming.)

Glen Rose isn't exactly bustling with activity, but you definitely want to take the time to visit **Fossil Rim Ranch**, which is one of the best drive-through exotic animal ranches in the country. Its rolling pastures and forests are home to many rare and endangered species whose survival is insured by the Fossil Rim Conservation Organization. Take an hour or two and roam the "veldt" of Central Texas.

Recently opened, the **Texas Amphitheatre** presents "The Promise" every weekend from mid-April through October. A professional cast of eighty members perform a musical portrayal of Jesus Christ's life. Featuring elaborate sets by Peter Wolf and costumes by Irene Coree, the play is very popular. Other varied performances will be scheduled when "The Promise" is not showing.

Up at nearby Granbury is the famous **Granbury Opera House** with its fabulous renditions of Broadway musicals and other productions. It doesn't matter what's on the playbill—it will be excellent.

So, if you love exotic animals, are fascinated by dinosaurs, want to see fine drama, or just want a romantic getaway, Inn on the River and Glen Rose has them all.

UTOPIA ON THE RIVER

P.O. Box 14
Utopia 78884
512-966-2444

Hosts: Polly and Aubrey Smith

Accommodations: 12 rooms.

Rates: $$

Location: Go west on Highway 90 from San Antonio. At Sabinal, take 187 north. Just a few miles south of Utopia, you will see the signs.

Amenities: Swimming pool, Jacuzzi, hiking, full breakfast, gift shop with local crafts.

Texas' Utopia began in 1852 when William Ware settled in the northeast corner of Uvalde County and named his town Waresville. Attempts were made to change the town's name to Montania, but in 1886 residents finally settled on Utopia because of the area's ideal climate.

Today Utopia is one of those places that you'll miss if you blink. Nor is the Sabinal River spectacular. It's only fifty-eight miles long before it joins the Frio. The Spanish named it for the cypress trees that line the banks. Yet, here on the edge of the Hill Country are some very special places.

Nestled on the banks of the Sabinal River is Utopia on the River, a small motel-style resort. All of the rooms are furnished alike in a sort of country-western decor. Some have small microwaves and refrigerators. A full country breakfast is served in the huge main room and reception area. For total relaxation, go out back to the pool and Jacuzzi. The pool is heated and can be used all year.

You won't find a row of restaurants in Utopia or in any

other town in this part of Texas, so you might want to pack a cooler and picnic.

The setting for Utopia on the River is wonderful. The area is covered with grand old live oak trees, but one is very special. The Storybook Tree was used to hide children during Indian raids. Polly and Aubrey Smith know all about this land because it has been in Polly's family since 1892. Polly will point your way to the dinosaur tracks along the river and tell you about historic sites on your hike. You have to hike the river! It's not good tubing here, but the hike is marvelous. For tubing Polly says **Conrad's Trading Post**, which is just down the road, is the place to go. You can also rent horses just down the road from the resort.

Note: All of the counties in this area are dry, so if you want alcohol you'll have to bring it.

THE WOODLANDS INN RESORT AND CONFERENCE CENTER

2301 North Millbend Drive
The Woodlands 77380
713-367-1100

Accommodations: 268 guest rooms and suites.

Rates: $$$

Location: 18 miles north of Houston Intercontinental Airport on I-45, exit Woodlands Parkway.

Amenities: 3 golf courses (54 holes including a PGA Tournament Player Course), pro shop, 24 lighted tennis courts, 2 full health spas, lounge, 2 restaurants, 2 swimming pools, racquetball club, game room, 40 miles of woodland trails, shopping center, conference center, special weekend packages.

Just off the fast lane of I-45 is the slow lane at one of Texas' most beautiful resorts, The Woodlands. Actually, The Woodlands also includes office buildings, private homes, shops, and the Cynthia Mitchell Pavilion, which hosts outdoor performances of top-name stars. But The Woodland Inn, tucked away among the dark pine trees, rests on the shores of Lake Harrison and overlooks the gently rolling fairways of three championship golf courses.

The guest lodges, each with 16 rooms, offer privacy and a special retreat amid the forest. Relax and take in the scenic beauty from your private balcony. A stay here is sure to energize you and restore your spirit.

Even the best golfers are tested by the North Course's mixture of tight fairways, sand traps, water, and woods. The Tournament Players Course is the site of the famous Houston Open. So a golf package weekend is one you can really sink your spikes into.

World Tennis and *Tennis* rated The Woodlands Inn "one of the top fifty tennis facilities in the U.S." An exciting Tennis for Life weekend package will get you right into the swing of things.

If you just want a luxurious pampered weekend and some romance with that special someone, try the Deluxe Pampered Weekend package. You can set mind and body adrift in a gently bubbling whirlpool, sip an icy glass of bubbly, and dine on superb cuisine. What a treat, and you deserve it!

Explore the exercise areas and try out the whirlpools, steam rooms and saunas, massages, facials, or even indulge in a

Japanese bath. And to really tone up, talk to a staff member about creating your own exercise program. The ladies spa offers a full beauty salon and herbal baths.

You can do a few lazy laps in the pools, or go all out at the Swim Athletic Center, practicing your swan dive or jack-knife into a diving tank from either the 5-, 7.5-, or 10-meter diving board.

After all that exercise you are sure to be starving. Choose from a lavish buffet of appetizers, entrées, fresh bakery selections, and tempting desserts in The Woodlands Room. Or, for that intimate dinner in an elegant setting overlooking the lake, choose from the Glass Menagerie's gourmet menu.

Antique lovers will enjoy another benefit of The Woodlands. The resort isn't far from **Old Town Spring**, where shoppers can browse in 82 quaint shops filled with odds and ends, arts and crafts, and snacks. This section of old restored houses are crammed in close together, so you can park your car and stroll at leisure.

The Woodlands is an oasis of comfort and style where outstanding recreational activities and deluxe accommodations are available in a naturally beautiful setting.

HORSESHOE BAY
COUNTRY CLUB RESORT

P.O. Box 7766
Horseshoe Bay 78654
800-252-9363 (Texas)
800-531-5105

Accommodations: Single bedrooms, condominiums, and private homes.

Rates: $$$ to $$$$

Location: 5 miles west of Marble Falls on Ranch Road 2147.

Amenities: 54 holes of Robert Trent-Jones designed golf, 2 golf clubhouses, Yacht Club, 2 swimming pools, 6,000-ft. lighted airpark, group facilities, 14 tennis courts, marina, fishing, all water sports, jogging trails, Equestrian Center, 3 restaurants, golf and tennis package weekends, temporary memberships for non-club members.

Restrictions: Dress code for all facilities, cancellation by certified letter only.

Located in the heart of the famous Llano Uplift, one of the oldest geological formations in the world, is Texas' premier luxury resort—Horseshoe Bay. Dotting this 4,000-acre expanse are facilities and amenities as fine as you'll find, anywhere else in the country.

Horseshoe Bay offers accommodations that match the elegance of expensive homes at The Inn, The Beach House, and the Hide-A-Ways. All are skillfully designed to blend with the natural beauty of the Hill Country and Lake LBJ.

The golf courses, called Slick Rock, Ram Rock, and Applerock are favorite destinations among a number of Texans.

None of these courses are for the faint-of-heart; Applerock was named by *Golf Digest* as the "Best New Resort Golf Course in America." The Cap Rock Clubhouse boasts a spectacular 70-mile view from its Grill and Lounge. Both Ram Rock and Applerock play out of this fully equipped shop.

Award-winning Slick Rock (6,839 yards, par 72) has 71 sand traps and water hazards on 12 holes, but it is considered the easiest of the 3 courses. The Ram Rock (6,946 yards, par 71) course is known as the "challenger" with its narrow fairways and rolling penncross greens surrounded by 62 deep sand traps. For sheer difficulty, Ram Rock is the main choice. Designed around brooks, waterfalls, and rock gardens, the course is also a scenic delight.

The newest course is the breathtaking Applerock (6,999 yards, par 72). Set in high, rocky terrain, the course demands well-placed drives and accurate club selection. *Golf Digest* described it as "rough, rugged and rustic in a beautiful way."

Tennis is not just a game at Horseshoe Bay, it is an event! Players are absolutely overwhelmed when they enter the imposing Tennis Club building. In addition to the pro shop, lounge, and spa, you find one of the loveliest water gardens in Texas. Lush foliage, sculpture, and statuary enhance the fountains, waterfalls, and sparkling pools. Even if you have never held a tennis racket in your life, you will find the water garden a lovely spot to ease jangled nerves.

For you joggers who hate to miss a daily run, lace up your running shoes and trot on out to the Fitness Trail. Distance markers are color coded for your convenience.

Think of a four-billion-year-old granite outcropping (give or take a few million), a 30-foot waterfall, black marble basins, and sand beaches, and you have captured the swimming experience at Horseshoe Bay. Both pools are landscaping gems. The 2-level Cap Rock Pool is limited to adults only. For family fun, try the Yacht Club Pool.

As you would expect from a resort with so much natural beauty, the horseback trails are an equestrian's dream. At the Equestrian Center, you can saddle up for a few lessons. Or you can bring your own mount and board it at the Center.

The deep blue waters of **Lake LBJ** are sure to beckon boating enthusiasts. Horseshoe Bay's full-service marina is equipped with 325 slips to house your boat. In addition to providing maintenance and repairs, this marina has a showroom with the latest in boats and accessories for sale. The folks at Horseshoe Bay won't overlook anything that will make your stay one to remember.

It's not DFW International Airport, but the Horseshoe Bay Airpark is still impressive with covered automobile parking, red carpet service, aviation gasoline and jet fuel, and a pilot ready-room.

With 28,000 square feet of elegance, dining at the Yacht Club is an artistic event featuring The Captain's Table, The Fairwind and Harbor Light, and The Keel Way. The Captain's Table is the most elegant of the three dining areas and requires reservations and proper evening attire. The Fairwind is more casual and The Keel Way features a young adult menu.

Horseshoe Bay's slogan, "The Standard by which all others are compared," describes exactly what awaits you.

Y.O. RANCH

Box 1H
Mountain Home 78058
512-640-3222

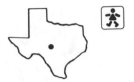

Accommodations: Rustic lodging for 35.

Rates: $$

Location: I-10 west of San Antonio. At Mountain Home, take Hwy. 41 south.

Amenities: Wildlife tours, walking trails, horseback riding, swimming pool, Jacuzzi, racquetball, handball, tennis, liquor store for guests.

Restrictions: One telephone, no television, reservations only.

To experience the Y.O. Ranch is to experience the history of Texas ranching and the era of the cattle barons. Back in 1880, when Captain Charles Schreiner acquired his original 550,000-acre domain, all he saw were waves of grass, some mesquite trees, and herds of ornery cattle called Longhorns.

These descendants of domestic cattle were lean and mean; a cougar thought long and hard before jumping on those lethal horns. In his heydey, Captain Schreiner (Texas Ranger, banker, Confederate officer) drove more than 300,000 head of those critters to Dodge City to amass his fortune.

The tough steaks from those Longhorns were soon replaced by fat, tender Herefords, and the historic breed almost became extinct. In the 1950s, Charlie III founded the Texas Longhorn Breeders Association which now boasts 3,000 members and more than 62,000 registered Longhorns. As Charlie says, "Without this rangy breed, there wouldn't have been a Y.O."

It was also during the 1950s that the Y.O. suffered a seven-year drought. The Schreiners wisely determined that another source of income was vital if the ranch were to survive. So, the Y.O. is world renowned for its exotic game hunting program and offers year-round hunting of axis and sika deer, aoudad, mouflon and Corsican sheep, and fallow deer.

Yet, the Y.O. is one of the leaders in exotic animal preservation. Experimental herds of ibex, barasingha deer, oryx, eland, addax, zebra, ostrich, giraffe, zebu, emu, and rhea also inhabit these Texas hills—to be viewed and photographed only. The Y.O. is larger than all of the zoos in the world combined, and many species may depend on ranches like the Y.O. for survival.

Precious water doesn't gush from springs on the Y.O. It takes 52 windmills pumping constantly to keep the water flowing for the ranch's 10,000 animals. Thus, the Y.O. is a working ranch in the truest sense. Along with the care and feeding of all the exotics, domestic cattle have to be herded, roped, branded, and fed. Cowboys on the Y.O. know what hard work is all about.

Tours leave at 10 A.M. every day except Christmas, and for two wonderful hours you are treated to viewing the Y.O.'s exotics. Then it's back to the Chuckwagon Restaurant for that hearty, delicious cowboy cooking. But you don't have to go home now. You can linger a day, a week, or a month. Across from the pool is a large meeting room called the Lodge. Attached to it are four modern guest rooms with baths. In back of the Lodge are five historic log and stone cabins, each with a bathroom, a stone fireplace, and air conditioning. You can also have your choice of twin or double beds. One flaw however is that the cabins have extremely poor lighting, so you won't be able to finish that book you read by the pool.

For a moderate fee per night, you can become a member of the Y.O. family. The price includes three hearty cowboy-style meals a day, unlimited use of the pool with its steaming Jacuzzi, and the wildlife tour at almost half price. Horseback riding is extra.

Please don't think of the Y.O. as a dude ranch. There are no organized activities other than the wildlife tour. David Schneider, Y.O. tourism director, says, "Basically, guests are on their own and can entertain themselves."

You won't attack your meals with the same fanaticism as Junior, the corn-loving aerobic ostrich, but you will utter a few moans and groans of ecstasy when you scoot your chair away from the table after a Y.O. feast.

During the summer there's plenty to do in the Hill Country at night. Enjoy the professional shows at the **Point Outdoor Musical Theater** in Ingram and then slap leather at **Crider's Saturday Night Rodeo** in Hunt. Check with the Kerrville Chamber of Commerce, because this is a swinging area with plenty of events going on all year. But, save some time to just sit and gaze at the billions of stars on those clear Hill Country nights.

One event you should really try to attend is the Y.O. Social Club party in early September. Billed as "the greatest party in Texas," people come from all over the country just to attend this soiree. Headline entertainers such as Willie Nelson and Jerry Jeff Walker are on stage. Celebrities such as Dan Haggerty, Ben Johnson, James Drury, and Peter Brown are also on hand to sign autographs. As for the food, you won't believe the variety of special dishes. Try the white wing dove, oysters Ernie, avocados and caviar, frog legs, and barbecued exotic game. Or, there's good old Tex-Mex and German food if you choose. You'll find a bar at every turn, a huge dance floor, and getups from worn jeans to Neiman Marcus apparel. Gates open at 7 P.M. and you head home after a monster Texas breakfast at 7 A.M. Get your tickets early because once they are sold out, they are sold out. Call 512-238-4277.

As the Y.O. is a hunting ranch as well as a working ranch, a getaway is not recommended during the hunting season.

GUADALUPE RIVER RANCH

P.O. Box 929
Boerne 78006
512-537-4837

Accommodations: Small dorm-style rooms to deluxe two-room cottages.

Rates: $$ to $$$

Location: Take FM 474 eight miles north of Boerne.

Amenities: 2 swimming pools, sauna, Jacuzzi, tennis courts, jogging and hiking trails, exercise equipment room, river tubing, horseback riding, aerobics, massages, small conference facilities, full American Plan.

On a bluff high above a bend in the beautiful Guadalupe River, in the heart of a Texas Hill Country live oak forest, is a ranch like no other. Here at Guadalupe River Ranch you will find a place to renew the mind, body, and spirit—you have found the perfect escape.

When you arrive at Guadalupe River Ranch, walk over to the swing overhanging the steep cliff at the edge of the lawn. Sit a few minutes and soak up the wonderful view. Down below, the clear river winds through the massive cypress trees, and as the breeze gently pushes the swing, you can hear the cows in the pasture on the opposite bank lowing with what can only be contentment in such a bucolic setting. Who cares what the rest of the ranch is like—the swing alone is enough to leave a fantastic memory.

The owner and creator of all this beauty is the author of several books on metaphysical subjects (*This Double Thread, The Ultimate Revolution*). Walter Starcke (STAR-key) also earned his fame as co-producer of several Broadway plays (*I Am A Camera, Cabaret*). This fifth-generation Texan returned to his home state in the 1970s and began looking for "about five acres of land" along the Guadalupe River.

When Walter bought this 380-acre ranch (that's a tad bit over the five acres he was originally planning on), the whole place was in the last stages of rack and ruin. Back in the 1920s, a San Antonio banker named Walter Napier sought an idyllic retreat for a summer home, and he found his paradise here on the Guadalupe. Napier built a magnificent home and even hauled in tons and tons of dirt to cover the rocky limestone and provide a foundation for the ranch's manicured grounds.

Napier's 8,000 sq. ft. home had suffered the ravages of time, that's for sure. It took a man with vision (and money) to see the possibilities for this ramshackle mansion. Starcke preserved the original mansion with a few changes, but did install the modern convenience of air conditioning. Several of the dilapidated outbuildings were removed, along with the water tower for the artesian well.

Before Starcke, and after Napier, the ranch passed through several owners. During the late 1930s, it was a hideaway for the famous movie star, Olivia De Havilland. According to the legend, Miss De Havilland backed her Cadillac limousine into a rock and became so infuriated that she sold her hideaway immediately after.

In the 1950s, the property was christened with the name of Golden Fawn Dude Ranch. Several masonry cottages were built for guests, and are still delightful with their screen porches, comfortable furniture, and bar facilities. Even in midsummer the breeze can be so cool that air conditioning is unnecessary. Starcke added a whimsical touch by naming the cabins for artists and scientists. You may be quartered in the Georgia O'Keeffe, Carl Jung, or Walt Whitman cabin.

A stone staircase (exactly 100 steps) leads down to the clean green waters of the Guadalupe River. Hike along the banks covered with dense vegetation and you'll find ancient dinosaur tracks embedded in the limestone. Even dinosaurs, with their pea-sized brains, knew a good spot.

Tubing here is without a doubt the best in Texas. Gone are the bumper-to-bumper crowds, so you practically have the river to yourself. If you forgot your tennies, don't worry. Up at the main house is a huge box of old tennis shoes for you to scrounge through in search of a pair your size.

So much adds to the restful ambiance of the Guadalupe River Ranch—the scenery, the setting, the accommodations—and then there's the food! Every meal is a dining experience. Fresh herbs from the garden enhance each dish. Many days the weather is so inviting that lunch is served al fresco under the trees. Dinner may be salmon steaks grilled over mesquite and topped with spiced herb butter, with side dishes of stir-fried carrots and green beans. Your day will probably begin with a heavenly omelette, tomatoes au brusso, new potatoes, and home-made wheat bread. Every meal just gets better.

So much superb food may make you lazy, but who cares? If you have guilty feelings over all those calories (even though the meals are well-balanced and actually very healthful), arrange for a horseback ride or an aerobics class. Jogging, hiking, or some laps in the pool may also ease those guilt pangs. And you can wind up all that exercise with a massage to sooth the sore muscles.

Then comes the best time of the day. It's back to the swing with an ice cold glass of champagne. If someone else had the same idea, there's a hammock big enough for two. It's a bit difficult to maneuver the champagne glass in a hammock, but not impossible. As the shadows deepen, you realize what a truly wonderful day you have had and are so glad that Walter Starcke had the foresight to create this idyllic retreat.

If I rated these Great Escapes, Guadalupe River Ranch would have a handful of stars.

FORT CLARK SPRINGS

P.O. Box 345
Brackettville 78832
512-563-2493

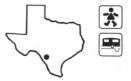

Accommodations: 38 motel rooms.

Rates: $$

Location: Highway 90, 123 miles west of San Antonio.

Amenities: Spring-fed swimming pool, spa, pool tables, horse stables, 9-hole golf course, 18-hole golf course, RV park, picnic area, restaurant and lounge, free cable television, museum.

If you are a Texas history buff, Fort Clark Springs is the perfect getaway for you. Your motel room is in the original 1872 stone barracks, so you can still relive life in a frontier fort with all the comforts the pony soldiers never dreamed of.

The active span of most of Texas' forts was very brief, but Fort Clark survived long after the threat of Indian warfare was over. Named for Major John B. Clark who was killed in the Mexican War, the fort was activated in 1852. It was June of 1944 before the fort's closure was announced, and 1946 before the last soldiers left its parade ground. For centuries past, this was the favored campground for the Comanche, Mescalero Apache, Kickapoo, Lipan and other tribes because of the huge, pure springs pumping 680,000 gallons of water an hour to create Las Moras (The Mulberries) Creek and a true oasis in a barren land.

It was here at Fort Clark that the famous Seminole-Negro Indian Scouts were stationed under the command of Lt. John L. Bullis in the 1870s. During their entire campaign not a single scout was killed, and four received the Medal of Honor. Fort Clark was the base of operations of Colonel Ranald S. Mackenzie's raids into Mexico to punish renegade Indians. The fort also served as the post for the black troops, whom the Indians christened "Buffalo Soldiers" for their tight curly hair.

As the years went by, Fort Clark built a roster of soldiers that would go down in the annals of American history. General George C. Marshall became U.S. Chief of Staff during World War II; Jonathan M. Wainwright became the hero of the Bataan Death March and Corregidor; and George S. Patton's bold armored operations in North Africa, France, and Germany are immortalized in World War II textbooks.

During WWII Fort Clark became a German prisoner-of-war camp, and when the fort closed, it was sold to Brown & Root Company of Houston for salvage and used as a guest ranch. Finally, in 1971 the property was purchased by North American Towns, Inc. and began to operate as a delightful residential area and resort.

All recreational facilities and guest rooms are available to visitors. Patton and Bullis Halls, two-story barracks built in the 1930s, are modern motel rooms with private baths, two double beds and color televisions. However, the rooms do not have telephones, so you'll have to use the pay phone outside.

The expanse that once heard the commands and bugle calls of troups is now a 9-hole, 3-par golf course open to the public. Also on the manicured and shaded grounds are tennis courts, a picnic area, stables, and another 18-hole golf course. The horses belong to the residents, but guests are welcome to bring their own mounts.

A dam on Las Moras Creek forms one of the best swimming holes in Texas—if you like a *very* invigorating dip, as that pure unchlorinated spring water is a constant 68 degrees. Lifeguards are on duty, and there's plenty of room to get in a number of laps in this gigantic pool. Las Moras Creek is also a favorite spot for fishermen and bird-watchers.

The old Officer's Club is now a newly refurbished restaurant and small bar. The food is good inexpensive West Texas fare with great chicken fried steaks.

Don't miss the fort's museum, now housed in the guard house, one of the oldest buildings on the post. The "drunk tank" is now filled with memorabilia of days long past when the only thing a soldier had to show for a month's pay was a night in this cramped cell. The "Empty Saddle" statue is a life-size riderless horse symbolizing the end of the cavalry. Ruins of the old fort cemetery are here, but the Seminole Indian Scouts are buried west of Brackettville on FM 3348. It was against post rules for Indians to be buried on the fort's grounds. The headstones do indicate the Medal of Honor scouts.

While life at Fort Clark Springs is far removed from the city lights, there's still plenty to do. Unless you flew in on your private jet to the resort's air strip, you should stop on the way down to Fort Clark Springs in Uvalde at the **John Nance Garner Museum**. Garner was the first Texan to be elected to the Executive Branch as Vice President under Roosevelt in the 1930s.

Just 7 miles north of Brackettville on FM 674 is the famous **Happy Shahan's Alamo Village**. Maybe you'll be lucky enough to see the camera roll and the stars in action at this location for western movies and television series segments. Founded by the great John Wayne and Happy Shahan for the epic movie, "The Alamo," the set has been added onto by other Hollywood and television productions. Many of the stars that faced a six-shooter on the streets of Alamo Village have autographed their photographs for Happy, and they are on display at the cantina. During the summer, bad guys and good guys shoot it out in scheduled performances, and a band entertains in the cantina while you enjoy a snack and soft drink. Longhorns bellow in the corral, and an authentic stagecoach will give you a ride around the Village.

About 30 miles west of Brackettville are the border towns of **Del Rio** and **Cuidad Acuna**. Del Rio's **Val Verde Winery** has been growing grapes for over 100 years, and is definitely the oldest winery in Texas. Val Verde's port wine has won numerous awards, and all of the wines are for sale. The grave of the legendary Judge Roy Bean is located on the grounds of the **Whitehead Museum**. He was well known for practicing his strange version of justice at his saloon, **Law West of the Pecos**. Del Rio was also the home of another character—Dr. John R. Brinkly—whose mansion is just down the street from the winery. Brinkly made millions during the Depression convincing old men that his goat-gland transplant would make them frisky again.

Acuna's main thoroughfare is lined with shops filled with

Mexican arts and crafts where you never know what treasure you might find. You will definitely find the best margaritas on the border at **Mrs. Crosby's** and the best meals at **Lando's**. Both are on the main drag and both stay open late. Lando's has a protected parking lot, so don't worry about driving your car across the Rio Grande.

After you leave Fort Clark Springs, hopefully you'll head west to see the **Davis Mountains** and **Big Bend National Park**, two more of Texas' great getaways. But, you'll always remember Las Moras Creek and its historic fort.

LAKEWAY RESORT AND CONFERENCE CENTER

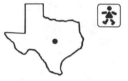

101 Lakeway Drive
Austin 78734
512-261-6600
800-LAKEWAY

Accommodations: 338 rooms at The Inn at Lakeway, Hill Country Villas, private homes.

Rates: $$ to $$$

Location: Take Highway 71 west from Austin to FM 620 and turn north. From Austin, approx. 20 miles.

Amenities: Full-service marina, 54 holes of championship golf courses, Jack Nicklaus-designed Academy of Golf, 32 tennis courts including one with a 1,200 seat arena, 3 swimming pools, horseback riding, hiking and jogging trails, airport with 4,000 ft. runway, hotel, restaurant, club, villas, conference center for 350, Camp Lakeway (ages 5–12), vacation packages, holiday packages, seasonal rates.

Below the pool deck, the Hill Country spreads out forever, offering a gorgeous view. Gray-green hills, sprinkled with resort homes, rise above the dark blue water of Lake Travis. A cool breeze blows away the sun's heat and lethargy is definitely the order of the day. Out on the golf courses and tennis courts players enjoy their games in perfect weather as water skiers zip across the lake. I found contentment by just stretching out on a lounge chair and watching a wren feed her nestlings. After every feeding she gave a beautiful rendition of a wren aria, fitting in perfectly with the world of Lakeway.

Lakeway began back in 1962 and was an instant success. Houses sprouted up like weeds on the limestone hills. Some were just weekend retreats, others were permanent homes, but all were top quality. That clean air, that clear lake water, the challenging golf courses, and spectacular sunsets— Lakeway has what it takes to be a sure winner.

Even in the hard times Lakeway survived and kept growing. Now FM 620 is four lanes lined with shopping centers, gas stations, and restaurants. But escape the whizzing traffic, and you meander your way through quiet residential areas to the Inn at Lakeway. Note the signs along the way, because you will want to come back to the golf courses and other activities.

The April, 1989 issue of *Business Week* picked its eight top resorts where spring arrives early or winter never comes at all. Lakeway was right up there with The Cloisters and Pebble Beach. *Business Week* particularly liked Lakeway because of its Jack Nicklaus-designed Academy of Golf and the World of Tennis, both top-notch instructional facilities. *Travel South* magazine has also given Lakeway rave reviews. The 167-yard No. 7 on the Hills Course, with its jagged yet carefully created waterfall, is postcard material and one of the most photographed holes in the country. *Travel South* also praised the Academy of Golf, which PGA star Tom Kite called "the number one practice and training facility in the country."

Tired of your spouse or special friend spending hours on the fairway without you? Why not take lessons at the Academy of Golf and beat your partner at his or her game. The academy has three full-length golf holes: a par 3, a par 4, and a par 5. All have multiple pin locations, 500-yard double-ended driving ranges, and practice greens. You can chip and pitch until you are putt-putt perfect. And even if your shelves are lined with golf trophies, various clinics are held by the nation's top instructors so you can add even more trophies. This academy was a pioneer in concept and design, and other resorts are following suit.

The World of Tennis has a solid reputation as one of the finest tennis facilities in the country. Anything a beginner or professional tennis player could want is right here. After all, if World of Tennis is good enough for McEnroe, Connors, King, Goolagong, Evert, and Navratilova, you should find it superb. Whether you opt for private or group lessons, you are guaranteed a top-notch instructor. After a hard workout on the court, what could be more refreshing than a dip in the pool—shaped like a tennis racket, of course.

For water sports, you have all of 65-mile-long **Lake Travis** at your disposal. Whatever you want to rent or launch is available at the marina, where you can also buy tickets for a cruise on the **Flagship Texas**. You can even invite 249 fun-loving friends to go with you on your cruise.

Want to hit the trail? You can saddle up, ride about 25 miles of trails around Lakeway, and arrange to treat your group to a good old cookout at the end of the ride.

While the golf and tennis facilities may get great reviews, Lakeway has plenty of other activities. The jogger will find paths to huff and puff around, and the Fitness Center has the latest weight equipment, a whirlpool, and a sauna.

Lakeway offers several options for accommodations. The Inn rambles over the hills with motel-style stone buildings that blend into the rugged landscape. Each room has a wonderful view of the lake with either a patio or balcony to watch the moon cast its liquid reflection on the water. Redecorated and refurbished, some of the rooms have the added convenience of a fireplace and kitchenette.

From the bar and large dining room in the main building, you can watch the water skiers slalom gracefully on the water and parasailers hover colorfully behind speedboats. Besides a standard menu, a buffet breakfast is served daily. Lunch is light fare, and at dinner you might choose the Inn's Sunset Menu. If you have dinner before 7 P.M., the charge is almost half price.

Villas are clustered around the tennis courts, and even though they are privately owned, they are in the rental pool. All are completely equipped and overlook the Hill Country. Also scattered throughout the resort are privately owned homes available for rent, with 2 to 6 bedrooms. So what's your choice? Take your pick from over 300 rooms and make your stay absolutely perfect.

A new treat for parents and kids is **Camp Lakeway**. For $20 a day kids are taken on trips to **Sea World** and other scenic spots in the Hill Country and given classes in all of Lakeway's sports and activities including golf and tennis. They also get lunch and a Camp Lakeway T-shirt. So, from 9 A.M. until 4 P.M., parents can relax and enjoy their activities knowing the kids are well supervised and busy. Camp Lakeway lasts from Memorial weekend until Labor Day.

Everyone cherishes the Texas Hill Country with its sweeping vistas, its gorgeous wild flowers, and its friendly people. There's no better place than Lakeway to experience it all.

INN OF THE HILLS RIVER RESORT

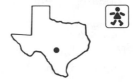

1001 Junction Highway
Kerrville 78028
800-292-5690 (Texas)
512-895-5000

Accommodations: 150 rooms, 67 riverfront condos.

Rates: $$

Location: Take Highway 39 from Kerrville to Hunt. Take FM 1340 west from Hunt for about 5 miles.

Amenities: 4 swimming pools (1 Olympic-size, heated), tennis courts, family sports center with complete facilities, restaurant, lounge, ladies spa, sailing, fishing, canoeing, paddle boats, putting green, golf nearby, small (maximum capacity is 300) convention center.

If there were ever a famous Hill Country tradition, it has to be Kerrville's Inn of the Hills. Folks have been coming to this rambling motel-style inn for over a quarter of a century. The atmosphere has always been like that of a mini-resort with its numerous activities, a good restaurant, and a lounge featuring live entertainment. Some rooms are hidden and tucked away, or you can choose a cabana with a poolside patio, or a suite.

Now something new and wonderful has been added to the Inn of the Hills—The River Club with 67 condo suites perched on the banks of the Guadalupe River is Kerrville's only luxury resort on the river. The river widens here, creating a calm lake setting, and as long as it isn't motorized, you can put anything that floats in the water. So, how about a dreamy moonlight canoe ride? Or if romance isn't what you're looking for, all sorts of fun crafts are available for rent.

You may want to try a dip in the Inn's heated Olympic pool, but the River Club has a gorgeous pool of its own, plus lighted tennis courts. And, for a *really* refreshing swim, try the clear waters of the Guadalupe, which have a fairly constant temperature of 72 degrees.

Just across the street is the adjoining Family Sports Center for all guests at the Inn. Here's an indoor pool, plus all the other health and fitness activities you could want. Even if you're an exercise wimp, you'll still love the Center's spas and saunas.

Suites at the condos have wonderful balconies overlooking the river that provide the perfect spot to enjoy an early cup of coffee or a late afternoon drink. Lovely furnishings, television, phone, a tiny kitchen, and a gorgeous view make the River Club's condos very popular with the Inn's guests. The River Club has its own restaurant, which is open for lunch, dinner, and a Sunday brunch. Candlelight on the tables and moonlight on the water make this a very special dining spot.

Over at nearby Ingram is the open-air **Summer Point Theater**, which performs Broadway musicals from June through August. The Inn offers a terrific theater package which includes two days and one night at the Inn, tickets to the show, and a pre-show dinner at the River Club.

Around Kerrville are lots of kids' camps. But why should kids have all the fun camping? So the Inn decided to create a camp where adults can enjoy the fun too. Totally non-structured, you don't have to sign up for any classes or lessons. There's no application fee, no deposit. Just show up! You have a choice of tons of activities; some for adults, some for kids, some for both. Many are free. You can take swimming lessons or learn to sail that boat you've dreamed of owning.

If you want to get out and see the countryside, but don't

want to hassle with driving and directions, the Inn has escorted tours all over the Hill Country. Just ask at the **Camp Information Center**.

Kerrville is home of **The Cowboy Artists of America Museum** where living artists keep the memories of the Old West alive. And just up at Mountain Home is the wonderful **Y.O. Ranch** with its guided exotic game viewing tours.

Check the Kerrville Calendar of Events and you'll find something fun every month. Around these parts the hills really are alive with music, for Kerrville hosts the best music festivals in Texas. Another really smashing festival is the **Texas Arts and Crafts Fair**, which is held over Memorial Day weekend. The best artists in the state show their talents in every artistic field.

Kerrville and the Inn of the Hills, with its River Club, are right in the center of the Hill Country and make an ideal location for an ideal getaway.

TAPATIO SPRINGS

P.O. Box 550
Boerne 78006
512-537-4611

Accommodations: 88 rooms, also condominiums available.

Rates: $$ to $$$ (Winter rates from mid-October to February 28.)

Location: Exit Johns Road off IH 10, 25 miles west of San Antonio.

Amenities: Swimming pool, four lighted tennis courts, sauna, Jacuzzi, exercise rooms, 18-hole golf course, restaurant, club, and conference facilities.

Tapatio Springs (Dancing Waters) is nestled in a beautifully secluded valley, and was formerly known as the Thunder Valley Ranch. Keep your eyes on the narrow country road as you wind your way to this secluded resort, but make sure to look for the gorgeous wildflowers, the wild turkeys, and the elusive white tails.

The resort dates back to 1980 when Clyde Smith purchased the Thunder Valley Ranch. Smith then realized his dream of combining a country club, conference center, and residential development. The luxury hotel features oversized rooms fitted with 2 queen beds, and a bar and restaurant that overlook its fabulous golf course.

Designed by Bill Johnston, Tapatio Springs Golf Course is a 6,666 yard, par 72 layout. A number of small lakes have been integrated into the course and provide its most challenging feature. Be prepared to contend with water on 12 holes. A bonus executive, par 34, 9-hole golf course is tailor-made for the leisure golfer. **The Blue Heron Invitational** is held in September and entries are limited, so make a reservation for this exciting golfing challenge early.

On Sundays, be sure to partake in the **Champagne Sunday Brunch**. Renowned for its abundant and delicious choices, the brunch attracts many local residents as well as guests. Dinners require casual attire, but gentlemen must wear shirts with a collar. Wine enthusiasts will love Tapatio Springs' wine list. You may order all those fine French wines, but you'll also find Texas wines featured. Live entertainment and dancing are provided Thursdays through Saturdays during dinner, and special holiday parties are held throughout the year.

Great golf, fine dining, and relaxing music are all yours in the enchanting land of the "dancing waters."

APRIL SOUND

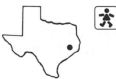

1000 April Sound Blvd.
Highway 105 West
Montgomery 77356
409-588-1101

Accommodations: Townhomes and hotel rooms.

Rates: $$

Location: 10 miles west of Conroe on Highway 105 on Lake Conroe.

Amenities: 27-hole golf course, 17 tennis courts (4 covered), 3 swimming pools, heated Jacuzzi, restaurants, lounge, marina, conference rooms.

April Sound is a golfer's paradise with a 27-hole golf course rolling over heavily wooded terrain. The course is divided into an 18-hole championship course that plays 6,100 yards and a 9-hole executive course. Golfers line up along the driving range and as they hit their shots, balls drop out of the sky and splash into the lake—on purpose. The resort has a lakeside range equipped with floating balls that are scooped up each day.

With six miles of shoreline on beautiful **Lake Conroe**, water sports are a natural option for fun. Sail your own rental sailboat or enjoy the sights from a guided powerboat. The lake is well-known for its excellent bass fishing, so bring your tackle.

Dining in the Ascot Room in the clubhouse is absolutely delightful with its view of the golf courses and Lake Conroe. All meals are prepared with the freshest ingredients. The popular Driftwood Club adjoins the Ascot Room and is the home of excellent libations.

One of the best parts of April Sound is the land itself. The tall dark pines and sparkling lake waters help you forget that busy routine and enjoy some badly needed quiet moments. Take a walk in the woods or set sail on the lake for a perfect sunset.

Just down the road, and farther west, is the quaint little hamlet of **Montgomery** with its antique shops and historic homes. Be sure to read the many historical markers that dot the town. In Conroe you will find the wonderfully restored **Crighton Theatre** presenting stage plays and musicals. And just south of Conroe, off I-45, is **Old Town Spring**, which is filled to the brim with antique shops, restaurants, and craft stores housed in vintage buildings.

GARDEN VALLEY RESORT, INC.

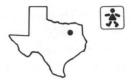

Route 2, Box 501
Lindale 75771
903-882-6107
800-443-8577

Accommodations: Condos and chalets, 64 guests.

Rates: $$ to $$$

Location: Adjacent to I-20, 17 miles northwest of Tyler, 80 miles east of Dallas. Exit at State Hwy. 110.

Amenities: Swimming pool, tennis, fishing, 36-hole golf course with a par 71. Restaurant, snack bar, lounge, golf packages, billiards, waterskiing, ski school, ski school packages, jet skiing.

Garden Valley is the fun-oriented creation of Bob and Martha Jackson and their son, champion water-skier John Jackson. Not only does Garden Valley offer all the traditional resort facilities but it also has a spectacular 38-acre lake designed and built by John Jackson for waterskiing and boat racing. This nationally-ranked slalom skier is head of the Garden Valley Water Ski School. So, if you want to become a water ski expert, or if you just want to manipulate a graceful slalom, you can learn that too. Best of all, any age is welcome.

You check in late Sunday afternoon and by Thursday you can slalom, trick, jump, and ski barefoot—well, maybe you can do all that if you train hard. You don't have to bring your own skis unless you prefer. A private on-site home, complete with 3 full baths, living room with fireplace, kitchen, and dormitory-style bedrooms houses the ski students. Meals are provided, and you can bet everybody is very hungry after hanging onto a ski tow all day.

Every day is "specials" day at Garden Valley for the golfers. And there's a special twilight rate every evening. The fourth hole, par five, is one of the toughest. From tee to pin it climbs 580 yards up a long narrow fairway to the flag at the top of the hill. Here is a challenge, even on your best days.

The chalets have woodburning fireplaces and full kitchens but you have to bring all your cooking supplies. Condos are luxurious with their vaulted ceilings, fireplaces, Jacuzzis in the master bedrooms, patio decks, and full kitchens. Kitchen utensils and an outside grill are provided. Some are 1-story, and the rest are deluxe 2-story condos.

One of the homes on the resort is listed with **Bed & Breakfast Country Style** in Canton (903-567-2899) and it comes with a moonlight canoe trip, but you do your own paddling.

The restaurant is open from 8 A.M. to 5 P.M. during the summer months and 8 A.M. to 4 P.M. the rest of the year. The adjoining club is open from 8 A.M. to 7 P.M. during the summer months and 8 A.M. to 6 P.M. the other months of the year.

Even though the resort is not grandiose or ultraposh, you can tell it is very popular with folks in East Texas. So if your interests include golf, tennis, waterskiing, or just finding a place in nature, Garden Valley offers the escape you have been looking for.

COLUMBIA LAKES COUNTRY CLUB, RESORT, AND CONFERENCE CENTER

188 Freeman Blvd.
West Columbia 77486
800-231-1030 (Texas)
713-757-3131 (Houston)
409-345-5151 (Local)

Accommodations: For 300 in multi-bedroom guest houses and lodge.

Rates: $$

Location: Highway 288 south of Houston, turn west on 35.

Amenities: Championship 18-hole golf course, Olympic-size swimming pool, lighted tennis courts, boccie and croquet courts, marina, bicycle rentals, lake fishing, deep-sea fishing, fitness center, large and small meeting rooms, exercise room, jogging trail, restaurant and bar, vacation and golf packages.

The scenery is lush and green down around West Columbia, and Spanish moss drips lazily from ancient oak trees. The historic **Brazos River** empties into the Gulf nearby. From September to December of 1836, West Columbia was the capital of the Republic of Texas. But accommodations were inadequate for the new Congress, so the capital was moved to Houston. On December 27, 1836, Stephen F. Austin died in this historic town.

West Columbia sort of slumbered through the years, but on January 15, 1918, the Tyndall-Hogg Well No. 2 proved lucrative, producing about 600 barrels a day and making millionaires of Governor James Hogg's descendants. Miss Ima, his daughter, dedicated her life to the enrichment of Texas, and one of her gifts was the restoration of the **Varner-Hogg**

Plantation at West Columbia. It is open to the public and is definitely a must see while visiting the area.

After the oil boom, West Columbia settled into its little-Texas-town identity. Then the mammoth Dow Chemical Company moved to the Texas Coast at Freeport. The entire area became a part of the industrial giant and life was never the same again. Yet, West Columbia still maintains its small-town status in spite of progress.

So even if you come to Columbia Lakes to play golf and just have fun, there's a bit of Texas history to savor and enjoy too.

The perfectly manicured golf course was designed by renowned golf architect Tom Fazio, and players declare it's a true test of golfing skill. Columbia Lakes is one of the first four locations in the United States chosen by the Niklaus organization for the Niklaus-Flick Golf School. The school counts among its staff celebrated golf instructor and sports personality Charlie Epps.

Nestled behind the course's berms are modern guest houses with 2 or 4 bedrooms that open off a central living area. A full kitchen is included but you have to bring your own utensils and supplies. Linens for bedrooms and baths are also included. If you have time to watch television, that's provided too. In addition to the cottages there is the attractive lodge, a two-story building adjacent to the Racquet Club and the Columbia Lakes School of Golf.

Non-golfers can sit in the yard and watch the players swing their clubs or go over and try a game of boccie (boch-e). The Romans loved it and you may, too. It's played with four balls weighted unevenly on each side. The object is to roll the balls so they end up as close as possible to the "jack," a small white ball thrown out at the start of the game. Each ball that is closer to the target ball than the nearest ball of the opposing team scores 1 point. All you have to do is get closer 16 times faster than the other team and you win. Or there's always the old favorite—croquet.

Columbia Lakes sponsors all sorts of activities for its guests, no matter what their age. You can count on plenty of golf tournaments, even a senior club championship, and tennis matches can be arranged. On Labor Day weekend the big contest is how well you can wield that ancient Filipino weapon, the yo-yo. So if you are ready to go "around the world," "walk the dog," "skin the cat," or "loop the loop," be at Columbia Lakes Cantina on Labor Day.

As for food, there are all sorts of special events. Their gourmet dinner of the month includes four courses of delicacies for about $27.50 a person and is a real bargain. Or, how about a complete dinner of salads for about $6.00? (But they don't promise them to be low-calorie.) Some days the resort goes bananas. All day long you can try a banana burger, banana bread, banana daiquiries, and even just bananas au naturel. The Top Banana award goes to the one who can eat the most bananas in 60 seconds.

The restaurant and bar are located in the large clubhouse, which has complete conference facilities. This is also a perfect setting for large parties and dances.

If you want to hit the beach for a change of pace, you can reserve a Columbia Lakes private beach house on the ocean. It has 2 bedrooms, 1 bath, and sleeps 6. It should cost about $250 a weekend. If you just want a day at the beach on your own, **Surfside** is only 25 miles away, so you will still have plenty of time for a late afternoon golf game.

Columbia Lakes' climate is a real draw. It is a very rare day when you can't hit the links or bat a few balls on the courts. In fact, the winter months may just be the best time to visit. But no matter when you plan to go, you'll love it all.

LAGO VISTA
COUNTRY CLUBS

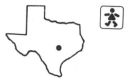

P.O. Box 4871
Lago Vista 78645
512-267-1121

Location: Take Highway 183 north, then left on FM 1431 and follow the signs. Maps will be mailed on request.

Amenities: Two country clubs, three golf courses, locker facilities and pro shops, marina, houseboat rentals.

The three superbly planned golf courses, located right next to each other, present an exciting challenge for any golfer, and the view of Lake Travis and surrounding hills adds to the special appeal of these courses. The demanding, par 72 Highland Lakes Course is 6,664 yards of gorgeous fairways and beautiful scenery.

The original golf facility and the club members' favorite is the picturesque Lago Vista Course. The 6,611 yard, par 72 course is a comfortable challenge to most golfers.

The Bar-K is a par 27, 9-hole executive golf course running about 2,200 yards long. The Bar-K is great for all levels and features relaxing waterfalls and wooded grottoes. Holes play from 90 to 230 yards, and each hole is a unique challenge.

VISTA GRANDE RESORT AND CONFERENCE CENTER

1918 American Drive
Lago Vista 78645
512-267-1161
800-288-1882

Accommodations: 1- or 2-bedroom condominiums, full kitchens, microwaves, or hotel/studio rooms.

Rates: $$

Amenities: Golf, water sports, tennis, skeet and trap ranges, restaurant, American Plan dining offered, lounge, playground, pool.

Restrictions: No pets.

Note: Vista Grande guests have visiting privileges for Lago Vista's facilities.

THE INN ON LAKE TRAVIS

1900 American Drive
Lago Vista 78645
512-267-1102
800-252-3040 (Texas)

Accommodations: 54 rooms.

Rates: $$

Amenities: Golf, water sports, free tennis, volleyball, shuffleboard, horseshoes, boat launch, full Lago Vista Country Club privileges, restaurant, lounge.

Both The Inn on Lake Travis and Vista Grande are small resorts that are immaculate and located right on the lake. While not ultraluxurious, rooms are spacious and most have a lake view. All guests have country club privileges at either Highland Lakes Country Club or Lago Vista Country Club. About 30 minutes from downtown Austin, you can easily have the city lights or total relaxation on the Lago Vista peninsula.

As with most resorts, home sites are available and many guests find Lago Vista an excellent retirement spot.

WATERWOOD NATIONAL RESORT AND COUNTRY CLUB

Waterwood Box 1
Huntsville 77340
409-891-5211

Accommodations: 84 lodge and cabana guestrooms.

Rates: $$ to $$$

Location: Take Texas 190 east from Huntsville 18 miles or 190 West from Livingston 21 miles. Enter gate and go another 7 miles.

Amenities: 18-hole USGA championship golf course, pro shop, golf packages, marina, all water sports, four swimming pools, health club, convention facilities, four tennis courts, and all outdoor court games.

When the Trinity River was dammed, it created one of Texas' largest lakes nestled in a beautiful setting with tall, dark green pines surrounding its miles and miles of shoreline. Lake Livingston's 90,000 acres had the potential to become the Lake Travis of East Texas, but somehow this never happened. A few nice subdivisions were built on the shores and a few adequate motels opened, but Lake Livingston became the proverbial fisherman's paradise and has remained that way.

Fortunately, the lake also has one perfectly beautiful resort—Waterwood. Halfway between Livingston and Huntsville on U.S. 190 is the striking entrance to the Waterwood world of extraordinary natural beauty and tranquility. Don't drive too fast as you enter because families of roadrunners make this parkway their home.

You know you are heading for a special place as you make the long drive into the deep woods. It may be rather a shock to see small street signs, but people do live on this side of Lake Livingston.

Prominent signs lead to the marina, condominiums, and golf course.

The Cabanas and Lodge offer beautifully designed guest rooms with patios and balconies overlooking the golf course. Or you may prefer rooms on Pools Creek Park, secluded hideaways with all the luxury of any of the guest rooms. All have very reasonable rates.

If golf is your game, the 18-hole USGA championship course is one of the top six courses in Texas. The Waterwood hole that players seem to remember above all others is "The Cliffs." This 225-yard, par 3 hole is rated by many golfers as the toughest water hazard they have ever played. Some golfers never go back, but others would rather play it ten times and get one good score than get good scores nine times out of ten on an easier course.

You can work on your backhand on four lighted tennis courts, or how about a dip in one of four pools? Don't forget your workout at the Waterwood Health Club with hydraulic weight equipment, saunas, and aerobic classes. And, don't forget the 90,000 acres of water inviting you to enjoy a number of water sports.

You'll find that the elegant Garden Room is a gorgeous

setting for leisurely meals with fine cuisine and attentive service. For cocktails, there's the adjoining Garden Court Lounge. Both have wonderful views of the golf course and surrounding forests. Fat ducks and geese waddle complacently across the grounds, and amateur bird-watchers can just sit on their balconies and start counting the large variety of birds that live in this part of the forest.

In addition to golf tournaments, Waterwood offers bridge nights, a dinner theater, special events on holidays, and just about everything that easy living entails.

RAYBURN COUNTRY RESORT AND COUNTRY CLUB

P.O. Box 36
Sam Rayburn 75951
409-698-2444

Accommodations: Hotel and condominiums with 1-, 2-, and 3-bedroom suites.

Rates: $$ to $$$

Location: Take U.S. 96 north from Beaumont through Jasper and turn east on Highway 255. Signs are easy to follow.

Amenities: 27-hole golf course, four lighted tennis courts, Olympic-sized pool, dining room, lounge, sports activity room with all games including a pool table and electronic games, golf packages, conference facilities, hiking and jogging trails, all water sports.

"Welcome to Rayburn Country!" These signs begin to appear among the tall piney woods of East Texas as you head toward Sam Rayburn Reservoir, the largest man-made lake to lie entirely within Texas' borders. With a 560-mile shoreline located in five counties, you can bet you'll see a lot of "Welcome to Rayburn Country!" signs.

As all Texans know, Rayburn was the beloved Sam Rayburn, Speaker of the House for 25 years. When President Johnson made the dedication of the dam in 1965, Johnson called Mr. Rayburn his teacher and counselor. "Speaker Sam" rose bushes are planted at the flag pole near the dam.

For the dedicated bass fisherman (or even an amateur) Sam Rayburn Reservoir is the place. It has a reputation as one of the best bass lakes in the country, and bass tournaments are held there all year. Rayburn Country can provide full fishing gear and a professional guide to show you where the big ones hide. You can try your skill for a half day or from dawn to dusk. Reservations are required and refunds are only given to those who cancel 24 hours in advance.

Breathtaking views of pine forests and lush fairways become an integral part of your accommodations. Spacious villas and hotel rooms afford complete privacy, yet all are within strolling distance of the resort's facilities. Some of the condos are right on your favorite No. 9 fairway, and others are down by the lake. All have modern furnishings, a small kitchen, and a queen-size sleeper/sofa in the living room. Beautifully landscaped, the condos blend in with the woody hill they rest on. Floorplans are included in the resort's publicity package.

Tee time begins on a 27-hole championship course designed by master golf architects Robert Trent Jones, Jay Riviere, Bruce Devlin, and Bob Ban Hagge. The three "nines" (Blue, Green, and Gold) offer exciting challenges seldom found in one location. A 300-yard driving range and complete pro shop round out the resort's excellent golfing complex.

In addition to the gorgeous pool, game rooms, and playground, ask for a map of the nature trails. Hike these primitive, dense trails and get acquainted with the real hidden beauty of the flora and fauna of East Texas. You probably won't spot the rare ivory-billed woodpecker, but you will see shy wildlife and unusual plants.

After a day on the links or baiting your hook, it's time to relax in the Country Club's dining room and lounge. With a sweeping view of the golf course, you can watch the late afternoon golfers finish up their round. A diverse and excellent menu assures a memorable meal. From mesquite-broiled, fine-aged beef to an array of salads, sandwiches, and seafood, Rayburn Country promises superb dining.

Rayburn Country offers all of the amenities you expect in a luxury resort, plus a staff that works hard to make sure the guests really enjoy their visit.

LAGUNA REEF

P.O. Box 1119
1021 Water Street
Rockport 78382
800-248-1057 (Texas)

Accommodations: 1- and 2-bedroom suites and rooms.

Rates: $$ (Winter rates available from mid-September to May 1.)

Amenities: Private beach, swimming pool, 1000-foot fishing pier, complimentary continental breakfast.

If it could be said that Texas had an artists' colony, it would be at Rockport. The area attracts artists, bird-watchers, and a variety of other sea and sun lovers. With its mottes (wind-sculpted live oak trees clumped together) lining the shore, Rockport does have a special aura. These famous trees are the trademark for Rockport, and they look as though Paul Bunyan took his giant saw and ripped away the tops. Of course, we all know it was the eternal gulf wind that created these living artworks.

Visitors come to Rockport-Fulton for all sorts of reasons and many never leave. Artists stay on to paint mottes, and bird-watchers stay on to watch the birds migrating or nesting. Many visitors just stay on because they like it for no special reason whatsoever.

Weekend people cherish this small part of Texas. All of the tourist attractions of Galveston are missing; there's no foofaraw about its historic districts (about the only historic place is **Fulton Mansion**, which is well worth the visit), and the beach is just a nice homemade Rockport project. But both resort towns do have great seafood. **Charlotte Plummer's** is a Rockport tradition, as is breakfast at **The Duck Inn**. And for great food and fun, don't miss **The Boiling Pot**. Clean butcher paper is spread on your table, and watch out! Here comes dinner! Heaps of steaming crawfish, shrimp, crab, corn, and potatoes are dumped on your table and it's every man for himself. Messy? You bet! Heavenly? You bet!

No matter why you come to Rockport, you'll love it. A good time to go is from November through April because you can call up **Captain Ted Appell** (512-729-9589) and get a wonderful lesson on the dangers facing the beloved whooping cranes and the conservation efforts underway. His boat tours of the rookeries are fabulous, and if you never thought much about whooping cranes before, the whoopers become very wonderful indeed. Rockport has published a fine booklet titled "Birder's Guide To Rockport/Fulton." Pick one up at the Chamber of Commerce, along with all the other brochures on attractions in the vicinity.

Recently opened is the **Texas Maritime Museum**. Small but extremely well designed, the museum traces the history of the area's maritime heritage. You can't miss the museum, it's the strange building across from the **Rockport Art Center**. The Center stages its monster Rockport Art Fair in July, and you'll see the work of some of the best artists in the state on display. No T-shirts and geegaws at this art show—just first-class art.

But if you come in the summer there's still lots to do. And no matter what time of year, Laguna Reef is the best place to use as your headquarters. Opening in 1989, this small hotel is fairly new to Rockport, particularly when you consider that a lot of motels date from the 1950s and earlier. Rockport could easily claim the title of "Mom and Pop Motel Capital of Texas."

Sort of off from town, Laguna Reef is located on a small lagoon. Put on your old sneakers and wade out and explore the marine life in the clear water. It's too shallow to swim here, but it's a delightful walk. Fishermen will be out on the pier casting their lines even before daylight.

The decor of the hotel reflects the beauty of Texas' Coast. The furnishings are bamboo and wicker, and colors are coral, sand, and bay blue. Bay-front rooms have a wonderful balcony to watch the pink and golden sunrise, and the suites come with a fully equipped kitchen and icemaker.

Laguna Reef doesn't have the usual hotel restaurant and bar. It does serve a big continental breakfast in one of the small rooms off the lobby. Here is a quiet little resort hotel with tons of charm and a lot of restful relaxation.

SANDY SHORES

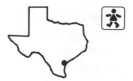

3200 Surfside
(P.O. Box 839)
Corpus Christi 78403
512-883-7456
800-528-1234 (Best Western)

Accommodations: 250 rooms.

Rates: $$

Location: Corpus Christi Beach

Amenities: Jacuzzi, pool, beach front, sauna, volleyball, a running course for joggers, and a Kite Museum.

Corpus Christi bills itself as "The Sparkling City by the Sea," and with that beautiful Shoreline Drive along the Gulf it really does sparkle. Corpus is actually a small town with a few skyscrapers, and the fast pace of Houston or Dallas just doesn't work in The Sparkling City.

Corpus is embracing the tourist business with its modern dog-racing track, **Maritime Museum**, the shops and cafés on Water Street, and its memorable **Dolphin Connection**. Erv and Sonja Strong have made friends with some of the most intelligent mammals on earth—the dolphins. You can go out on one of their two daily excursions into Corpus Christi Bay and experience a sight you'll never forget. You'll see Sonja and her admiration society of dolphins interacting like long lost best friends.

Sonja has named her buddies and knows all their personality quirks. With hugs and kisses and a fat slimy fish or two, this incredible woman and her dolphins show you why dolphins should be treated this way instead of being forced to perform in an aquarium show. Sonja is so glad that the **Texas State Aquarium** decided not to include any aquatic mammals in their exhibits. Studies have shown that captivity has a disastrous effect on these magnificent mammals' life span. For a trip of your lifetime, call the Dolphin Connection at 512-882-4126. It's not far from Sandy Shores.

East of those skyscrapers is the mile-long Corpus Christi Beach. The area is sort of funky with its motels, seashell shops, and some rather sleazy bars. But it is here that the marvelous Texas State Aquarium is located, and this is one of the outstanding attractions in the state. Phase I, completed in 1990, features the Gulf of Mexico and the exotic coral reef, the Flower Gardens. For more information on the Aquarium, call 512-880-5858.

The place to stay on the Corpus Beach is Sandy Shores. This resort isn't one of those giant hotels where you can never locate all the bars and restaurants, but it is the largest on the beach. Be sure to ask for a room facing the Gulf, and even though the balconies are a bit small, you still have room to sit out and watch the ocean sparkle. The annex is a motel-type building where rooms face the pool, sauna, and Jacuzzi. All rooms are extremely comfortable and attractive, but don't expect luxurious, expensive touches.

Before you head for the beach or the pool, take a few minutes to walk through the small, but delightful, **Kite Museum**. It's open 10 A.M. to 5 P.M. 7 days a week and admission is free. For centuries, kites have been floating in the breeze for all sorts of reasons. Some were flown for religious reasons, some for warfare, some for scientific experiments, but mostly kites are flown for plain old fun. At the end of the tour, stop by the gift shop and pick one of your own and go fly a kite!

Then you can join in a game of volleyball, take a dip in the gentle surf, or just sit in your beach chair and watch everyone else do those activities.

For joggers, Sandy Shores has printed a runner's guide. Miles are marked on the guide, and pros can cover 12 miles around the area.

The **Espresso Coffee Store and Restaurant** offers Columbian, Hawaiian, European chocolate, Espresso, and Cappuccino coffees. You can also purchase these exotic coffees by the pound. For that late or early snack, **The Pantry** will deliver pizza to your room or make it ready for pick up.

Don't miss the **Calypso Restaurant and Bar** and its wonderful view of the bay. A good time to stop in is during the complimentary wine tasting from 5 P.M. to 7 P.M. But that's not all, from 10 P.M. to midnight you can savor a rich Viennese dessert buffet. The Calypso has thought of everything for that perfect romantic evening.

Sandy Shores is only 5 minutes from downtown Corpus, yet it seems miles away in atmosphere and offers a special getaway in the heart of The Sparkling City by the Sea.

PORT ROYAL BY THE SEA

P.O. Box 336
Port Aransas 78373
800-242-1034 (Texas)
800-847-5659

Accommodations: 210 luxury beachfront condo suites.

Rates: $$$ (during high season: spring break, June through Labor Day.)

$$ (during regular and low seasons: April and May, September and October; November through mid-March.)

Location: Mustang Island

Amenities: Fully equipped kitchen, washer and dryer, swimming pool, restaurant, tennis, volleyball, game room, golfing nearby, surf fishing, meeting facilities.

Restrictions: No pets.

Port Aransas used to be a little fishing town and was about as close to a quaint seaside town as Texans could get. Back in the '30s Franklin Delano Roosevelt arrived to do a little tarpon fishing, and everybody in the country knew where Port Aransas was—for a few days. Well, the tarpon disappeared, and no other U.S. president put Port Aransas on his itinerary, but progress arrived anyway.

Today Port Aransas is still famous for its deep-sea fishing, and tournaments are held practically every weekend. But now fast-food stands and T-shirt and shell shops line the main drag. The seaside quaintness is gone, but the wonderful beaches on Mustang Island still make Port Aransas a great escape. Luxury condos line the beach, and all are excellent, but the crème de la crème in resort condominiums is at Port Royal By the Sea.

Beautifully furnished in modern rattan, each suite has a fully equipped kitchen with microwave, as well as a washer, dryer, wet bar, stereo, television, and phone. Many suites also include a steam bath.

Every suite at Port Royal has a balcony overlooking the beach or the beautiful 500-foot Royal Blue Lagoon Pool. This spectacular pool, dubbed the largest in Texas, features 4 whirlpool spas, which always have a soothing, not scalding, temperature. You can also enjoy the cool water as you sip your favorite drink at the swim-up cabana bars. A waterslide entertains the kids.

Tropical plants and a waterfall fill the landscape and create a setting reminiscent of a South Sea island. In the evening when that big Texas moon rises over the horizon, the Blue Lagoon Pool is absolutely breathtaking. It is open 24 hours, so why not take a romantic midnight swim, or a soak in one of the spas with a glass of champagne—in a plastic glass, of course.

This same gorgeous view can be seen from the penthouse restaurant. You have a full menu, bar, and good food, and when the moon is up and shimmering on the water, the view of the pool from the restaurant is worth the visit.

Probably the main reason you came to Port Royal is to while away carefree hours on the beach. A wooden walkway takes you over the dunes and down to the surf. Bring your own beach towels because the hotel doesn't furnish them. If you forgot your kite, there's a shop on the way to town that has them in all shapes, colors, and prices. Beaches and kites just seem to go together.

Even in the height of the season there's plenty of room to spread out on Mustang Island's beaches. You'll escape the beer joints, hot dog stands, and rental stalls, but the bad news is there's lots of the nasty, gooey tar that spreads insidiously over Texas' coasts. For your convenience (and please use it), the hotel has provided a cleanup station to get you back in your room without tracking tar on the carpet.

If city lights beckon, Corpus Christi is just a short drive over the causeway and offers dog races, The Texas State Aquarium, and plenty of fine restaurants. But, do try **The Pelican** in Port Aransas for great seafood and steaks. A sunset cruise around the area is also a real treat. For an escape where life is easy and the accommodations are perfect, look to Port Royal By the Sea.

LAS CAMPANAS GUEST RANCH

P.O. Box 238
Vanderpool 78885
512-966-3431

Host: Ernst Schneider

Accommodations: 5 rooms, 4 baths in Hacienda Las Campanas; one 3-bedroom lodge with full kitchen and fireplace.

Rates: $$$

Location: 35 miles west of Bandera on FM 187 north of Vanderpool.

Amenities: Photo safaris of exotic animals, fishing (catch and release), hiking, bird watching, lighted tennis court, swimming pool, Jacuzzi, volleyball, gourmet dining, cookouts, small seminars, 3200-foot paved landing strip.

Restrictions: No pets

When all is said and done, Las Campanas is way up on the scale of great Texas getaways. Out in the far reaches of the beautiful Texas Hill Country is a ranch totally different from the delightful dude ranches. Here you *and* the wildlife are pampered guests. Antelope, which originally roamed the veldt of Africa, make their home on Las Campanas' 2,500 acres. You'll see magnificent greater kudu and eland standing majestically in the brush posing for photos. A herd of white oryx, from the Sahara Desert, with their curving scimitar horns, perk up their inquisitive ears as your jeep drives by. Then they quietly return to chomping on that thick Texas grass. Black buck antelope from India butt heads and horns to determine which one will establish his territory as the dominant male. Mousy brown females hardly take notice of all this clacking of horns as handsome male black bucks spar in the meadow.

Meanwhile, over by the water hole, a herd of North American elk lift gigantic racks of antlers to check out the jeep before they casually stroll off into the brush. Silly zebras gallop past, a few waterbucks stare back, and all is right with the world at Las Campanas.

And this is what Las Campanas is all about—being right with the world. When the sun begins to sink behind the hills, it's time to grab your binoculars and head for the photo safari ride. You'll find that a lot of the exotics love to have their picture taken and are ready to ham it up. Ernst will cover a big portion of his reserve for you, and if Texas only had a few acacia trees, you'd think you really were in Kenya.

As dusk really settles in, it's time to head back to the beautiful Hacienda. Maybe you'll have time for a quick dip in the rock-walled swimming pool and its swirling Jacuzzi or for a set of tennis before dinner time. Dinner is served in the large dining room, and Ernst and his staff know exactly how to please hungry photo hunters. A steak grilled over mesquite, a piping hot baked potato, a hearty tossed salad, a fine chilled wine, and a superb desert make up just one of Las Campanas' excellent meals.

Then it is time for after-dinner music, and guests are really in for a treat. Ernst is an accomplished guitarist and has a large repertoire. Maybe you're fond of Willie Nelson, or Harry Belafonte, or Eddy Raven, or Ernst Schneider. Ernst not only plays, but composes his ballads as well. And if you haven't had time to strum your own guitar, play that sax, or toot that clarinet, bring it with you to Las Campanas and join in the music. On fine evenings, the music is out by the pool. When the weather is brisk, the music's around the fireplace where some of Ernst's colorful neighbors may join you.

You may find your eyelids getting heavy fairly early, but

that's fine. Here at Las Campanas, you make your own hours. However don't sleep too late, because after a quick cup of coffee in the morning, it's off to see the animals again. Ernst will probably head up into the high hills on the ranch where the trees and brush form deep woods, caverns, and ravines. Sometimes you may see more wildlife in the mornings than late evenings, so be sure not to miss the early safaris.

Then it's time for a Las Campanas breakfast with home-made German rolls, toast, juice, cereal, fresh fruit, boiled eggs, bacon, sausage, and lots of coffee. Before heading out for another day of fresh Hill Country air, take a few minutes and admire the decor of the Hacienda. Art treasures are everywhere with excellent paintings, fine carvings, bric-a-brac, and sculptures. Each of the large airy bedrooms also have special artistic touches that blend perfectly with the modern decor. The shower in one of the upstairs bathrooms is big enough for two, and the balcony overlooks the creek's swimming area.

Not far from the main Hacienda is the Lodge. Spacious and comfortable, with a big fireplace, a modern kitchen, a large living area, and three bedrooms that make it the perfect retreat for a small group.

Lost Maples Natural Area is just up the road. **Garner State Park** is just over the hill, and **Medina** with its famous apple orchards is the place to load up on apple cider, apple butter, apple pies, apple trees, or just some baskets of apples. You can choose between tubing on the Frio or the Sabinal Rivers, horseback riding at nearby stables, visiting the tiny museum in Leaky, shopping at the antique shops in the area around Uvalde, or just watching the monster catfish cruise the creek at Las Campanas. And the best part of all, is that no matter what time of year you come, the animals will be ready to pose and the scenery will be terrific. Those unforgettable moments truly occur here at Las Campanas.

Roamin' the Range
Dude Ranches

Bandera prides itself on being "The Cowboy Capital of the World," and it's true. This famous little town is known all over the world, and guests arrive from many foreign lands just to be Texas cowboys for a few memorable days. They want to ride horses and experience living on a Texas ranch. But many of the visitors to Bandera are from the good old U.S.A., and they want to do those very same things. Here in Bandera, the Texas mystique is alive and well.

Way back in the dark ages before there were interstates (actually about 1950) I went to Bandera for the first time. I can't even remember the name of the dude ranch where I stayed, but I've never forgotten the horseback rides, swimming in an ice water creek, and eating tons of good food. Bandera had just started working hard on a big reputation for a tiny town, and it has succeeded beyond its greatest expectations.

When the dudes aren't out riding on the ranch, they head for town to shop for souvenirs, antiques, and cowboy duds. At night they like to "skoot a boot" at the old (1934) **Cabaret Dance Hall**. Unknowns such as Willie Nelson, Faron Young, and the immortal E. T. once played the Cabaret for enthusiastic audiences. If your feet don't know about the Texas two-step, the Cabaret will provide dance lessons and you'll be stomping the Cotton-Eyed Joe in no time at all.

Across the street from the Cabaret and down a steep flight of stairs is a country-western fan's idea of heaven—**Arky Blue's Silver Dollar Saloon**. Lots of video games, pool tables, a long heavy bar, freezing cold beer, and Arky's band. What more could a Texan want for a good time?

For a picture of Bandera's past, visit the **Frontier Times Museum**. In 1720 the Spanish and the Apache met in a deadly battle that raged 3 days. Both sides were the losers, and the Spanish retreated to Mexico. A second battle between 40 Texas Rangers and 100 Comanches was fought in 1842, and this time the Rangers won. Bandera was open for ranching.

Guests with sporting blood will head for **Bandera Downs** where there's thoroughbred and quarterhorse racing from November 28 through February 28. The track has been completely overhauled, the computers set up, and from now on, it's "Place your bets, ladies and gentlemen." (512–796–7781)

What would a western town be without rodeos? These rough and tumble cowboy events are held throughout the summer with the big one every Labor Day weekend.

For some of the most scenic drives in Texas, turn to Bandera County. Elevations range from 1,200 to 2,400 feet as you wind your way up from the crystal-clear flowing river bottoms to the peaks that provide views of Mother Nature's most gorgeous efforts.

Bandera has 5 wonderful dude ranches that can give you a taste of western life. Each is unique in its own way, but all see to it that you have a perfectly marvelous visit. Meals are feasts fit for a king (and his queen), the invigorating climate makes you feel great, and your bed will

always be a welcome sight after a day of being a dude—
no matter which ranch you chose.

For more information on Bandera's dude ranches, write
the Bandera Chamber of Commerce at P. O. Box 171,
Bandera, 78003. Or call 512–796–3045.

MAYAN DUDE RANCH

P.O. Box 577
Bandera 78003
512-796-3312

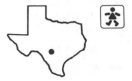

Hosts: The Hicks family

Accommodations: Western native rock cottages with 1 to 4 bedrooms. The Mayan Lodge, Log Cabin, and Hitching Post have connecting 2-room suites. All have private baths and color televisions.

Rates: $$

Location: The Mayan is just on the outskirts of town. You can't miss the signs, particularly the one at the entrance that reads, "There's no place like this place anywhere near this place, so this must be the place."

Amenities: American Plan includes three meals, two horseback rides daily, plus all activities. Pick up in San Antonio, tennis courts, swimming pool, hayrides, souvenir shop, lounge, tubing on the Medina River, cowboy breakfasts, hiking, workout room.

Restrictions: No pets. No 1-day reservations.

If there ever was a family business, it's the Mayan Dude Ranch. All of Don and Judy Hicks' kids and their spouses work very hard to make your stay at the Mayan the best vacation you ever had, and they do their job exceptionally well. You can't believe so many handsome Hicks! (Don and Judy have 13 children.) They sing, they dance, they work at every job, and they make the Mayan a perfect getaway. Since 1951 the Mayan has been catering to dudes, and guests return over and over again. The ones that can't go back every year wish they could.

The big rush season is from June through Labor Day. You need to make reservations wa-a-a-a-y in advance and an entire week is highly recommended. You'll love every minute of every day. At night there is a great selection of activities—a huge barbecue with ALL the trimmings, or maybe a Mexican Fiesta, or a Fifties Night, a Talent Night, country-western dance lessons, movies, gambling in the Mayan Gambling Parlour, special performances by the Hicks Gang, or an adult horseback ride to Booger Red's Saloon in Ghost Town.

You'll get an early start with a cool glass of fresh orange juice and some real cowboy coffee delivered to your room first thing in the morning. How's that for special treatment! Then get set for a massive intake of calories at the end of a horseback ride over a trail into the hills. It's dozens and dozens of eggs, southern grits (yummmmm!), hash-brown spuds, bacon cooked crisp and curly, homemade link sausage, and . . . yep, there's still more! You've got to have oven fresh biscuits, and then you need to waddle over and have the wranglers fix you a breakfast tortilla and tacos with mushroom, onion, cheese, and tomato concoctions. Mayan Lou, a gray-bearded veteran wrangler, will probably be serenading you with western tunes while you pig out. Note the artwork on his teeth. Lou has "Texas" written in gold on his top chops. Lou's dentist probably loved that job. If you can't get back on Old Paint after that feast, climb aboard the hay wagon and ride back.

While on the subject of food, lunch is usually served poolside with mountains of salads, fresh fruit, and a chilled glass of wine or some other long, cool drink. When you are seated in the dining room, you can see miles of hills and rivers in the clear, clean Hill Country air. A spacious deck adjoins the dining room and bar, and it makes a perfect place for that drink in the evening as you watch the sun's fireworks in the west.

A word of advice—maybe you better buy those new jeans a size too big. And when you're home and back at work, dreaming of all that fantastic fare, you can cook it yourself right from the Mayan's cookbook, *Miss Judy's Wild Western Recipes.*

One of the wonderful aspects of Mayan's plans is that there are no plans. The only activities you have to sign up for are the horseback rides. Other than that, you are on your own to roam the hills, tube the river, hit the pool, practice your backhand, mosey down to see the dinosaur tracks, or sit under a shade tree and finish that book you meant to read all year. Ladies are even treated to a pool-side luncheon and fashion show. So, choose your own brand of vacation—the "Mayan-way."

Cabins look rustic from the outside to fit in with the rocky Hill Country terrain, but they are modern and comfortable inside. You probably won't see much of your quarters, however, because there's so much going on at this fabulous dude ranch.

The Mayan knows that families have to come in the summer when school is out, but you really miss the best time of all if you can't spend some days in the spring and fall. You can enjoy all of the activities of the season, just not on a regular schedule. But, no matter when you visit, the Mayan promises warmth, hospitality, and relaxation—you get it all, and more!

DIXIE DUDE RANCH

P.O. Box 548
Bandera 78003
512–796–4481

Hosts: The Crowell family

Accommodations: Guest rooms and cottages, some with televisions and fireplaces.

Rates: $$

Location: From Bandera take Highway 173 ¹/₂ mile south and turn right on Ranch Road 1077—9 miles to ranch.

Amenities: American plan, horseback riding, swimming, cookouts, hayrides, cowboy breakfasts.

Restrictions: No pets, deposits refunded with 1 month cancellation notice, 2-day minimum stay.

Dixie Dude is the oldest of the resort ranches in the Bandera area, owned and operated as a working ranch by the same family since 1901. Since 1937, the Crowell family has been offering Hill Country hospitality and wants you to think of Dixie Dude as "your home on the range" with fabulous food and good family fun.

Lodging is in white-frame cottages with wagon wheel furniture and air conditioning. Some have fireplaces and televisions. The Round-Up Room in the headquarters building has a television, a juke box, and a piano.

Daily horseback rides take you up in the hills to some of the most scenic country in Texas. Beautiful vistas, smoky blue hills, and gigantic rock ledges make the Dixie Dude's trails the best of the dude ranch rides. Gentle horses and friendly wranglers add to the pleasure of the rides.

This old-time Western Stock Ranch is still a working ranch, and you can count on food fit for cowhands—very good and plenty of it. Dixie Dude offers ranching with comfort and pleasure at very reasonable rates.

LH7 RANCH RESORT

**P.O. Box 1474
Bandera 78003
512-796-4314**

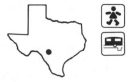

Host: Maudeen Martha Marks

Accommodations: 10 rock cottages with kitchenettes, RV hookups, camping.

Rates: $$

Location: 2 miles northwest of Bandera on FM 3240.

Amenities: Montague Lake for fishing, swimming pool, tubing, lodge, catering (minimum 15 people), entertainment arranged upon request.

The LH7 brand is particularly symbolic here in Texas because LH is an abbreviation for Longhorn and the numeral 7 represents the seven basic bloodlines recognized and preserved by breeders of Longhorn cattle. So not only is LH7 a guest resort for people who love the Hill Country and its attractions, but this working ranch is the proud home of purebred Texas Longhorns. Owner of the LH7, Maudeen Martha Marks, says she has two entirely different sets of clientele; there's the cattle buyers and the resort guests.

Maudeen's family has raised these famous Texas cattle since the 1840s. Her late father, Emil Henry Marks, is credited as one of the few ranchers involved with preserving the Longhorn.

Maudeen didn't plan to go into the resort business; she was just looking for a place to move her cattle from the family ranch in Barker. She believes fate led her to the perfect place in Bandera. Her ranch had originally been owned by generations of Montagues, and as a result, the family's symbol, Ms, is everywhere. To top it off, Lake Montague looks like the head of a Longhorn from the air. So, Maudeen and her herd moved west.

Lake Montague, regardless of its shape, covers forty acres and is stocked with bass, crappie, brim, and catfish. Fishermen love it. Cozy stone cottages with screened porches face the lake, and the kitchens are stocked with utensils for four. Linen service is also provided.

The lodge, Sala Grande, is a large stone building with a monster fireplace that makes it perfect for big parties. A rock pathway leads to the swimming pool that overlooks Montague Lake.

The beautiful, clear Medina River flows along one side of the LH7. Guests love a refreshing drift on inner tubes, or traveling up river to Blue Hole, which is legendary for its "big ones" and never fails to tempt the anglers. Even though the resort does not have stables, Maudeen can arrange horseback rides and hayrides.

Staying at the LH7 is a double experience. Not only can you have a great time being a dude, but you can also learn to appreciate how a real ranch works.

TWIN ELM GUEST RANCH

Box 117
Bandera 78003
512–796–3628

Hosts: Frank and Mary Anderwald

Accommodations: 21 rooms including rustic but air conditioned cabins.

Rates: $ to $$

Location: Ranch Road 470 three miles south of Bandera.

Amenities: American Plan, campfires, hayrides, swimming in pool or river, horseback riding, recreation area, Greyhound bus pickup.

Restrictions: 30 days notice for deposit refund, no pets, pay phone only, no meal on Sunday night, 3-day minimum stay, open March through Labor Day.

Twin Elm is also a working ranch in Bandera and is located on one of the highest peaks in the lovely Bandera hills. "We're a real down-home, casual place. A sort of 'mom and pop' operation," says Mary Anderwald, who is "Mom." "Pop" is Frank Anderwald, grandson of one of the original Polish families to settle in Bandera. He was a wrangler at the Twin Elm when he met Mary.

Frank and Mary have a large string of saddle horses, gentle and willing to amble along the tree-shaded trails on the Medina River. Twin Elm brags about its ranch cooking, and in good weather (which is most of the year) dining is outdoors. The ranch is famous for its barbecue and country biscuits.

If you want to have a great dude ranch vacation at a price you can easily afford, come to Twin Elm. The Anderwalds will be looking for ya.

SILVER SPUR GUEST RANCH

P.O. Box 1657
Bandera 78003
512–796–3037

Host: "Texas" Tom Winchell

Accommodations: 11 stone cottages.

Rates: $$

Location: 10 miles south of Bandera on Ranch Road 1077.

Amenities: American Plan, swimming pool, hayrides, cookouts, western entertainment, hiking, horseback riding, pack trips, deer hunting.

Restrictions: Minimum stay 2 days, 4 weeks notice for deposit refund, no pets.

Silver Spur, Bandera's newest guest ranch, opened in 1980. The main ranch house/dining hall perches on a hillside with a splendid view of the wonderful Texas Hill Country. This ranch specializes in horseback riding, and a friendly experienced wrangler will have you galloping off into the sunset in no time at all.

Also, you can become an ole cow hand and have a true ranch experience as you help feed the livestock, groom and saddle your horse, and perfect your riding skills. Old Paint could easily become your best friend, particularly after riding him twice a day.

Rooms have king size and double beds, private baths, and color televisions. But, best of all, they have a view of the whole outdoors. You can count on great ranch-style home cooking, and it's served in the Ranch House's spacious dining room.

Why did owner "Texas" Tom Winchell build a dude ranch when most of the others had been established for decades? Tom Winchell answers,

"I like horses and people, and that's basically what dude ranching's been all about from the beginning. Those things plus this special area of Texas."

FLYING L RANCH

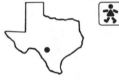

HCR1 Box 32
Bandera 78003
800–292–5134 (Texas)
512–796–3001

Accommodations: Completely equipped suites.

Rates: $$ to $$$ (children ages 3 and under stay free)

Location: Take Highway 16 north from San Antonio to Bandera. At the light, turn left on Highway 173, drive 1 mile, and there you are.

Amenities: 18-hole, par-72 golf course, pro shop, horseback riding, tennis courts, swimming pool and hot tub spa, sporting equipment, lounge, laundry facilities, pay phones, small conference center, package weekends, air strip (3,250 × 50), dance pavilion.

The Flying L ain't like the rest of the dude ranches. For one thing, it not only has an 18-hole, par-72 golf course, but it also has an airstrip with a mechanic and gasoline service. Pretty fancy for a dude ranch, huh?

The Flying L is not rustic or even western looking, but it sure has great western hospitality. Bordering the golf course's Ninth fairway are the new modern Golfview Suites. Each two-room suite comes with a kitchenette, television, and a queen-size sofa bed in the living room. Be sure to ask for one of the suites with a double-sized whirlpool bath. The spa out by the pool is large and wonderful, but there's nothing like having your own private little spa. Another special feature of each Golfview Suite is the private balcony. It's a great place to watch the golfers, have a cup of coffee, a late evening drink, and star gaze after the sun goes down. You can even see the deer as they wander over to nibble at those delicious greens.

Only a horseshoe pitch from the swimming, dining, and tennis facilities, the Flying L's Ranchview Suites are designed with fully-equipped kitchens, large patios, and make a perfect place for small get-togethers.

Villa Suites are nestled beneath huge live oaks, and if you aren't interested in frills, these 2- and 3-room units offer just about the best basics in Bandera, and many have fireplaces. So name your choice, pardner. You can have just what you want at Flying L.

If you came to Flying L for some horsing around, you can pick a mount from the corral and ride off into the sunset along the trails to San Julian Creek. Or how about riding off into the sunrise for one of those cowboy breakfasts that leave you so full you can hardly get back on Old Paint? Flying L cowboys know how to really show dudes a good time. And San Julian Creek is definitely a brisk alternative to the Olympic-sized pool, so toss your suit over your saddle horn and get your feet wet in the crick, as it's called in these parts. If you are a real tenderfoot and even gentle Old Paint looks too tough to handle, climb aboard the hay wagon and follow the crowd to that cookout.

Meals are served in the main lodge. You'd better bring along a hearty appetite for a real Texas-style barbecue with all the good stuff like corn on the cob, pinto beans, coleslaw, and potato salad. And what dude can resist the Fiesta Mexicana with all those Tex-Mex favorites . . . tacos, refried beans, tamales, fajitas. . . . Olé! Even an everyday breakfast in the dining room starts your day out right with scrambled eggs, butter-soaked pancakes, breakfast tacos, sausage, bacon, good ol' grits, hash browns, biscuits, and gravy. Now that ought to get you off to a fast start for a hard day on the range. Every meal at Flying L is a feast, but on Sunday the spread makes the table groan from the weight of all those dishes. You don't come to Flying L to go on a diet, that's for sure.

Golfers won't be disappointed on the Flying L's par-72 course. The ninth hole is a 441-yard, par-4 hole where accuracy off the tee is a must. The tight fairway is lined by trees on the left and an embankment on the right. Hole number seven is also a killer with water in front and to the right of the green.

When you register at this great little dude ranch you'll be given a schedule for all the activities. No matter what age the dudes are, there's plenty of fun awaiting you at the Flying L. As the folks at Flying L say, "Come join us for the land—lotsa land and lotsa fun."

PRUDE RANCH

P.O. Box 1431
Fort Davis 79734
915–426–3201
800–458–6232

Accommodations: Guest lodges, family bunk rooms, ranch bunkhouses, camp sites, full RV hookups.

Rates: $ to $$

Location: Highway 118 just west of Ft. Davis.

Amenities: Heated indoor swimming pool, lighted tennis courts, weight room, hydrotherapy spas, exercise room, television and lounge area, horseback riding, hiking, hayrides, convention facilities, summer camp for boys and girls.

Restrictions: For reservations refund, a 72-hour advance notice is required. No refunds for early departure. Meal tickets purchased from the office are required for each meal. Horseback riding is an extra charge.

No matter which way you drive into the Davis Mountains you will have to face the barren terrain without the taste of cool water. But when you reach this wonderful oasis, those long, dreary miles are more than worth the reward. Here the days are fresh and cool, the nights brisk, and the scenery fantastic. For a total rejuvenation of spirit, Fort Davis and Prude Ranch are all you need.

Fort Davis was established in 1854 to defend the gold seekers headed for California. Named for the Secretary of War, Jefferson Davis, the fort was the site of the Great Camel Experiment. The camels arrived and proved successful in the American desert. Then the Civil War erupted, and Jefferson Davis left his post to become President of the Confederacy. Many of the camels were turned loose, and the stories of strange humpback creatures appearing to desert prospectors were told throughout the West.

The fort has been authentically restored and many buildings are open to the public. During the summer, special programs are staged, and every 30 minutes a bugle's lonely wail is heard calling to the ghostly soldiers.

Fort Davis has several charming places to stay. The historic **Limpia Hotel** in town is furnished in antiques and has a wonderful porch to watch Fort Davis pass in review. On the way to **McDonald Observatory** is **Indian Lodge**, a comfortable adobe pueblo-style motel built during the Depression by the CCC.

But, to really experience the Davis Mountains and the Old West, you have to visit the Prude Ranch. Prude Ranch was established in 1898 as a cattle ranch, and even though it is currently run by the sixth generation of Prudes, it is still a cattle ranch. However, John Robert Prude has remained in step with the time's changes and converted part of his property to one of the best dude ranches in Texas.

Guest cottages feature spacious bedrooms, baths, and private porches with rocking chairs. Vaulted ceilings, Mexican tiled floors, and rustic ranch furniture add to the aura of life on the range.

Western-style bunkhouses can accommodate as many as 250 guests. In the bunkhouses guests must provide their own linens and towels. Dormitory-type bathrooms and cot-size bunk beds make the bunkhouses perfect for large reunions. Family bunk rooms have 1 double bed and twin-size bunk beds. None of the rooms have telephones or televisions, but pay phones and television viewing areas are located around the ranch.

Meal time brings cowboy breakfasts and chuck wagon

feasts. No matter where you chow down—in the dining room or out on a hayride—you'll love this excellent Texas down-home fare. Meals are individually priced and very reasonable.

The most popular area on the ranch is the horse corrals. Guests enjoy the open-range horseback riding as much as any activity available. The herd of horses numbers over 100, and many are registered quarter horses. You'll always find a special horse that is just right for you.

If you didn't get enough exercise on your horseback ride, you can bat a few balls on the tennis courts, swim laps in the heated pool, hike for miles, exercise in the workout room, or if you don't find any of these options appealing, you're welcome to help the wranglers with their chores. This is a working ranch, and the cowboys can always use a hand feeding the stock, rubbing down the horses, or saddling up the ponies.

Nightlife in the Davis Mountains does not include the theater, movies, discos, or big parties. Sometimes you can do some country-western two-stepping or maybe listen to a lecture on Big Bend. But since the stars at night are big and bright in the Davis Mountains, your best bet is to go to McDonald Observatory. Here you'll see the universe on parade. Most nights, the only thing you may want to do is hit the rocking chair or the bunk bed.

An amazing number of guests reach Prude Ranch and don't want to move too far away from the horsey aroma of the corral. However, even though you are in the middle of the Great Chihauhaun Desert, just an hour away by car is the colorful Judge Roy Bean's **Law West of the Pecos Museum**. Up at Marfa are the mysterious **Marfa Lights** (great balls of light that move across the sky). A word of warning before you go, the Marfa Lights do not appear on a regular schedule. You could wait for days, months, or even years. **The Museum of the Southwest** is on Sul Ross campus in Alpine, and the ghost town of **Shafter** is just up the road a piece.

A. G. Prude (1872–1940) wrote the following verse, and while it's not epic poetry, it does sum up Prude Ranch:

> Come to the Mountains
> Enjoy the pure air,
> Where the nights are cool
> And the days are fair.
> Five thousand feet—
> That's our elevation.
> 'Tis an ideal place
> To spend your vacation.

LAZY HILLS GUEST RANCH

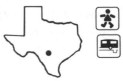

Box G
Ingram 78025
512–367–5600

Hosts: Bob and Carol Steinruch

Accommodations: 26 cabins.

Rates: $$

Location: From Kerrville take Highway 27 west to Ingram, turn right at light, drive 2¹/₂ miles.

Amenities: American Plan, Olympic-sized pool, hot tub, cookouts, tennis, archery, hiking, hayrides, fishing (bring your own gear), horseback riding, game room, deer hunting, RV hookups, playground, hot tub, off-season rates.

Restrictions: No pets, 3-night minimum stay in summer and during holidays, deposit returned with 15 days prior notice, no refund for early departure, horseback riding offered for an additional charge.

Open since 1959, this family-owned, 758-acre guest ranch is just 15 minutes from Kerrville. Bob and Carol Steinruch call Lazy Hills "the family ranch for folks of all ages." And their aim is to help folks feel at home in the friendly Texas Hill Country. You will find they accomplish that aim and then some.

With 30-plus miles of wooded hiking and horseback riding trails, well-stocked fishing tanks, an Olympic-size pool, and all sorts of court games, there's plenty to do at Lazy Hills. Kids addicted to video games will even find a game room. But most of the action is outdoors.

Even those who have never straddled a saddle before become at ease on the stables' gentle horses. Trails wind up and around tree-covered hills and down deep valleys, following rocky streams and climbing craggy mounds. You will love the scenery, but keep a watch for deer, wild turkeys, and other wildlife scurrying around in the dense brush.

All trails lead to the dining room in the big Brown Palace where the best home cooking in the Hill Country is served. Don't worry about calories, you'll be burning them up with the ranch's activities. Just chow down and enjoy. The cook will even pack you a hefty lunch for your day trip if you request it the night before.

Guest rooms sleep 4 to 6 persons and some have woodburning fireplaces. If you are coming in the winter months, a fireplace can feel mighty good. Don't expect to watch television, however, except in the central lounge.

Lazy Hills is so perfect that you may not want to leave the gates. However, Kerrville is a real nice town with its summer theater, Criders rodeo, and two-stepping. Plus, you must take a tour of the fabled Y.O. Ranch with its exotic game animals from six continents and the first registered herd of Texas Longhorns. Be sure to visit the **James Avery Showroom** in Kerrville and the **Cowboy Artists of America Museum**.

Those evenings at Lazy Hills, when you just kick back and watch the busy little hummingbirds in action, are great. But do venture out at least once to see more of the area.

It's in the Water
Spas

Spas are no longer the domain of wealthy women or aging actresses. Spas are now affordable. And for many, a spa is the ideal vacation. Not only can a sagging body be shaped up, but sagging minds get rejuvenated as well. Another big change in spas is that men are more than welcome, and programs are available for them as well as women. The all-female spa is almost a thing of the past.

Spas are different from the health club in the local shopping mall. For one thing, you stay on the premises, and every minute of every day yields something wonderful for your body and psyche. From an aerobic workout to a new hairstyle, spas cater to every facet of your well-being.

For years, a spa was referred to as a "fat farm," or considered a treatment center for alcohol abuse. Today, spas are designed for people with healthy attitudes toward their bodies. Still, for the majority of spa guests, weight loss and relief from stress are the main objectives.

In Europe, spas have been trying to boost their client's health for eons, but in the United States, spas are a new concept in the vacation business. Most people who would love a spa vacation feel they are just too expensive. But, with the emphasis on physical fitness, many

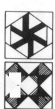

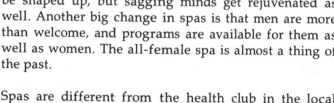
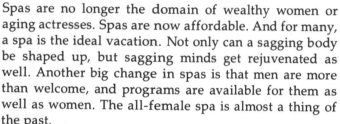

spas are lowering prices and courting a new clientele. However, the first spa in Texas, The Greenhouse, is still non-coed and still very exclusive.

If you are considering a local health club to continue your weight loss and exercise program, write to the following office and ask for their brochure, "Selecting a Health Spa," before you sign up:

Texas Attorney General
Consumer Protection Offices
P. O. Box 12548
Austin 78711

All of those machines and whirlpools can be a waste of money unless you know what you are getting with your membership. You also need to know your legal rights before you sign a contract with a health spa. Too many sleazy health spas and gyms bilked the public before the Health Spa Act was passed in 1985.

THE GREENHOUSE

P.O. Box 1144
Arlington 76010
817–640–4000

Accommodations: Private rooms and suites for 39 guests.

Rates: $$$$

Amenities: Total spa facilities in luxurious mansion.

Restrictions: Women only.

In Texas, the granddaddy (or is that grandmother?) of the spas is The Greenhouse, which is more than twenty-five years old. Not only is it one of the oldest, it is also one of the most luxurious and most expensive spas in the country. It began as a project of Neiman-Marcus, Charles of the Ritz, and the Great Southwest Corporation, catering only to the richest and most well-known women. A week at The Greenhouse in the 1960s was $750 and is now more than $5,000 per week. The prices may have changed, but The Greenhouse still only accepts women, preferably very rich and very famous women.

A typical day at The Greenhouse begins with a personalized schedule card on your breakfast tray. Then, exercise sessions are interspersed with facials, massages, various beauty treatments, and sauna and whirlpool baths. The luncheon is informal, but dinner is served in the formal dining room. Meals were planned by Helen Corbitt and have been updated to follow new dietary guidelines. Consuming about 800 calories a day is recommended for clients who wish to lose weight, and no alcoholic beverages are allowed on the premises.

The Greenhouse serves a maximum of 39 guests and employs 125 specialists to oversee their programs. Private rooms have luxurious baths and dressing areas, and private telephones. Suites are available as well.

Evenings are spent at seminars, fashion shows, discussions on health and nutrition, or relaxing concerts. During the week, time is allowed for a limousine trip to **Neiman-Marcus** to shop for a new wardrobe to go with the new you.

Most Texas spas have similar plans, and all are dedicated to physically and mentally revitalizing their clients.

THE PHOENIX FITNESS RESORT

**111 North Post Oak Lane
Houston 77024
800–548–4700
800–548–4701– (Texas)**

Accommodations: Luxury guest house, 15 persons maximum.

Rates: $$$$

Amenities: 3 pools, tennis, racquetball, full state-of-the-art spa facilities, specialized programs.

Restrictions: Men only allowed during "Coed Weeks," 1-month cancellation notice, less $100 cancellation fee.

Texas has two of the nation's premier spas. One is The Greenhouse and the other is the prestigious Phoenix. Nestled on a 22-acre wooded park, The Phoenix's grounds are shared by the nationally-known and exclusive Houstonian Health and Fitness Club, but your private accommodations are located in the club's intimate Ambassador House Hotel.

A typical day begins at 7:30 with dry cereal, fresh fruit, and skim milk. After a wake-up stretch, it's on to low-impact aerobics. You get a juice break, but it's not for long because you'll take a power walk. That massage feels great, and your spa cuisine lunch tastes wonderful after all that activity.

In the afternoon you'll enjoy water aerobics, a manicure, a Yoga session, and having your hair done. The cocktail hour is time to meet your fellow spa guests and chat over a nonalcoholic cocktail before another healthy meal.
No wild evenings of dancing and gaiety for you. You are here to heal your body. Your evening will include lectures on self-defense, nutrition, cooking, and exercise programs.

You can do this for 6 days during "Ultimate Week," a special stay that even includes a shopping trip.

The Phoenix emphasizes a fitness program that you can continue to follow when you leave, an ongoing workout and nutrition guide that will keep you healthy and feeling good.

HUDSPETH HOUSE AND SPA

1905 4th Avenue
Canyon 79015
806–655–9800

Accommodations: 6 guest rooms, 5 baths.

Rates: $$

Amenities: Gourmet breakfast, special programs, hot tub, exercise facilities.

Restrictions: No smoking, no pets.

On a less grand scale than The Phoenix or The Crescent is the historic Hudspeth House, out in the Texas Panhandle. The Hudspeth House is a charming combination of bed and breakfast inn and health resort. Mary Elizabeth Hudspeth came to Canyon in 1910 as one of the original faculty members for what is now West Texas State University. She boarded with the Turk family and fell in love with their home. In 1913, Mary Elizabeth bought the Turk house and moved it closer to the campus. Through the years, the teacher remodeled and decorated her home and shared it with her many friends, including Georgia O'Keeffe, another faculty member.

Now owned by Sally and Dave Haynie, the home offers inviting guest rooms decorated in antiques. Most of the guest rooms also have gas-burning fireplaces. Also, a very individual health and fitness spa has been incorporated with Hudspeth House. Two programs are offered.

The Daily Program includes a gourmet breakfast and a full-course low-calorie lunch, self-motivation classes, and a fitness and diet program. The computerized fat analysis determines your percentage of body fat, and a daily diet and exercise regime is planned specifically for you. Skin care and other beauty seminars are held, and the day ends with a luxurious massage and a soak in the hydro-therapy hot tub. A Swedish massage is extra.

The Weekly Program includes 5 nights lodging, gourmet breakfast, light lunch, and candlelight dinners. Self-esteem classes are held daily, in addition to all of the amenities of the Daily Program. Shopping trips and sightseeing tours are also part of the Weekly Program.

The goal of Hudspeth House is to pamper you as you become more assertive, healthy, and physically fit. With small groups (no more than 6 or 8 at a time) there is plenty of time for individualized attention. On staff are a doctor, nurse, cosmetologist, fashion consultant, masseur, and professional instructors.

The motto of Hudspeth House is: "Learn to love, laugh and live younger."

SPA AT THE CRESCENT

Hotel Crescent Court
400 Crescent Court
Dallas 75201
214–871–3200
800–654–6541

Accommodations: 190 rooms, 28 suites in luxury hotel.

Rates: $$$$

Amenities: Pool, private club, shopping at The Shops and Galleries of The Crescent, hotel guests may use The Spa.

Restrictions: Adults only.

If you wish to experience the elegance of nineteenth-century Europe with its grand hotels, majestic courts, and exquisite boutiques, all you need do is visit the opulent Hotel Crescent Court in Dallas. Surrounding you are graceful arch windows, travertine marble floors, and definitely a touch of Versailles without Marie Antoinette and King Louis. However, the Hotel Crescent Court is worthy of the greatest royalty and is where many stay while in Dallas.

The Spa at the Crescent is redefining the whole concept of a health spa, mixing the best of rejuvenating European treatments with American ideas of fitness and health.

Real men do have facials, even if you do call them skin treatments. At The Spa, the skin care program is the famous treatment of the Lancaster Beauty Farms of Baden-Baden and is the only place in the United States offering the full Lancaster program. Each person's skin is different, so The Spa offers an individualized program.

Light spa meals are aesthetically arranged on glass plates that don't absorb the light and color of the food, and all look and taste superb even when cutting those calories. The juice bar also offers a light refreshment that is nutritious.

The Spa bases its rejuvenating program on the spas of Europe with water therapy, massage, skin care, facials, body wraps, Swiss showers, and mineral baths. For strengthening and toning, individual trainers and private sessions are available. Special classes on sports stretching are offered and also Yoga and relaxation techniques. Don't miss those cold and hot tubs and that invigorating Swiss shower.

Locker rooms are complete with all the things you need to pamper your body—shampoos, soaps, and 100 percent cotton towels. You will be furnished with all workout clothes and robes.

Sometimes after a spa day you just want to lie peacefully, think of absolutely nothing, and let your body feel good. The Spa understands the value of this euphoric feeling, and encourages you to stretch out in a quiet room before leaving for the real world.

The intent of The Spa at the Crescent is to help you complete your journey into wholeness.

VERANDAH CLUB

Loews Anatole Hotel
2201 Stemmons Freeway
Dallas 75207
214-748-1200

Accommodations: 1,620-room luxury hotel.

Rates: $$$

Hours: 6 A.M. – 9 P.M. Monday through Friday
 7 A.M. – 8 P.M. Saturday
 8 A.M. – 8 P.M. Sunday

Amenities: Hotel guests are welcome for a small fee, weekend packages, full spa facilities, tennis, racquetball, squash courts, even a croquet court, indoor running track, 2 restaurants.

Restrictions: No set daily spa program.

Loews Anatole Hotel is the largest hotel in the Southwest, so it's no surprise that it offers one of the finest health clubs in the Southwest as well. You can come to Loews Anatole for a weekend or a year and never have to leave this city within a city.

Beside this incredible hotel lie seven acres of a peaceful green park crowned by a lovely mansion. It's the Verandah Club, a $12,000,000 world-class spa and sports center. And you can count on having every luxury, plus every facility a health and sports club can possibly include.

The Verandah Club's Socio Grill serves light, quick, and healthy meals as well as upscale gourmet entrees every day, and it's open daily as is the Verandah Lounge for cocktails.

Personal training, the health service of the '90s, offers one-on-one supervision and coaching for an additional charge.

But, you need more than just exercise. The Verandah Club provides a fitness assessment testing giving you the cold, hard facts on where your body needs help. And after you do that, have a reflatron cholesterol screening. Those light, healthy meals at the Socio Grill may become very important to your body.

Now the business traveler can take his workout on the road at The Verandah Club. According to *Shape* magazine, Loews Anatole is considered one of the top 10 health-conscious hotels in the country due to its fine fitness facilities. Special passes are available to The Verandah Club for the business-man who wants to keep his exercise program going, or just wants stress relief.

The Verandah's Eucalyptus Inhalation Room is the only one of its kind in the area. Every 15 minutes air is forced through an air compressor into a 5-gallon tank of eucalyp-tus oil, and the vapor and steam are jetted into the inhala-tion room. During pollen and flu season, the Eucalyptus Room is very popular and a great relief for allergy sufferers.

Another big treat for travel fatigue is the massage therapy. You can relax those weary muscles with either a Swedish massage, sports massage, shiatsu, trager, accupressure, or foot reflexology.

End your day with a stroll through the hotel's enclaves and admire the largest collection of art ever assembled for an American hotel, including: Picassos, second-century Khmer artifacts, one of the largest pieces of Wedgwood ever fired, a white marble gazebo, and a matched pair of 3-ton Thai elephants made from monkeywood.

FOUR SEASONS

4150 North MacArthur Blvd.
Irving 75038
214–717–0700

Accommodations: 315-room luxury hotel.

Rates: $$$ to $$$$

Location: In Las Colinas near Dallas.

Amenities: Two 18-hole golf courses, indoor/outdoor tennis, racquetball, indoor/outdoor pools, indoor/outdoor jogging tracks, squash courts, weight rooms, full spa facilities, hotel guests may use all amenities, Golf 'n' Spa packages.

Boasting unparalleled personal service and virtually every health and beauty treatment available, The Spa at the Four Seasons Hotel and Resort offers an experience available at only a few of the world's most luxurious spas. Just reading the brochure is a mind-lifting experience and makes you want to reach for the phone and dial for a reservation.

The Four Seasons says, "Our primary objective is for guests to be treated like kings and queens and leave the hotel with an invigorating and memorable experience."

As for the ultimate massage, The Spa offers Swedish, shiatsu, and aromatherapy massages. Swedish massage works with the major muscle groups on soreness, tension, and relaxation. Shiatsu is an ancient massage from Japan and emphasizes pressure on various points of the body tracing energy to the internal organs. Just as it sounds, aromatherapy employs oils and herbs to rejuvenate your body.

After a massage, it's time for the sauna and steam rooms, whirlpool, a cold plunge, and then perhaps a few minutes of sunshine on the outdoor tanning deck. But if you really want to take full advantage of The Spa, experience the Loofah (trade name) salt glow and herbal wrap treatments. The Loofah treatment begins with a full body massage using a mixture with salt to lift dead skin cells and stimulate circulation. Then, the massage is followed with a body scrub and shower treatment with an organic sponge and liquid peppermint soap. To wind it up and leave you totally limp and languid, try the herbal wrap treatment with linen sheets steeped in herbs wrapped around the body. All of these marvelous treatments are extremely effective in eliminating toxins from your body, or so the Loofah line states.

When you can move again, The Spa offers a full-service beauty salon and for the men a full-service barber salon. But perhaps you had rather sign up for an aerobics class, do a few laps in the indoor pool, or even take karate lessons.

The restaurants in the Four Seasons offer a delicious Alternative Menu with Spa Selections. The numbers in parentheses are the total number of calories you will get with that order. The Creamy Cauliflower Soup is a mere sixty calories, but you could really set a limit with the Duck Consomme at only ten calories. Instead of adding up how much money your meal will cost, add up the calories instead.

Not only is this an elegant hotel with wonderful views, The Spa is absolutely luxurious as well. Nothing has been overlooked that a guest might wish in the way of body tone-up. Naturally, most of the athletically inclined will prefer the sports arena with all the squash and racquetball courts and jogging tracks.

Check out some of the special weekends offered by the Four Seasons. You can choose one that emphasizes golf, one that is totally dedicated to The Spa, or even a golf 'n' spa getaway. If you couldn't care less about golf or The Spa, then try the Honeymoon Package. No matter which honeymoon you celebrate, here is guaranteed romance.

You will leave the Four Seasons Hotel and Resort feeling like royalty. Long live the king! And, of course, the queen.

LAKE AUSTIN RESORT

**1705 Quinlan Park Road
Austin 78732
800-847-5637 (Texas)
512-266-2444**

Location: Hwy. 71 north of Austin, then west on FM 620. Watch for signs and go 5.5 miles off FM 620.

Accommodations: 80 guests in 20 deluxe cabins, or standard hotel/motel rooms.

Rates: $$ to $$$

Amenities: Indoor/outdoor pools, gym, Jacuzzi, boutique, hiking trails, weight room, full beauty salon, paddle boats, and a secluded stretch of Lake Austin. Courtesy transportation from Austin airport.

Restrictions: No guests under 14 and guests 14 to 17 years of age must be accompanied by a parent.

As you drive down the narrow road to Lake Austin Resort, you find that the cares and woes that were dragging you down melt away before you've even checked in. The setting for this rejuvenation clinic is absolutely lovely. A contemporary motel-style building clings to the side of a hill, and the landscaping is vines, shrubs, and flowers growing profusely around rocks, decks, and stairways. A wide green, manicured lawn stretches to the lake, and on the lake's shore is the lodge with the dining room, living room, work-out rooms, and the indoor pool. This non-diving pool is designed for water exercises or a warm soak after the Jacuzzi. The outdoor pool adjacent to the lodge is more than large enough to swim some long laps and firm up the arms and legs.

Guests are able to tailor a fitness program to their own needs, and as in all spas, meals are nutritious and the emphasis is on fresh products. Lake Austin Resort also offers a marvelous cookbook filled with the resort's personal recipes. *Lake Austin Resort Recipes* is the effort of Deborah Evans, a director of Lake Austin in 1984, and this cookbook has since gone into several printings. No wonder, for all of the recipes are to encourage proper nutrition. It is amazing how food low in fat, salt, and sugar and high in fiber can be so delicious and so filling and yet not fattening. Meals are served at a set hour each day, and everyone is expected to be on time.

The living room and dining room are furnished with comfortable overstuffed sofas and chairs, and tables are loaded with magazines. The menu is posted on the dining room wall and includes the number of calories per serving as well as the fat and fiber content. So what you see is what you get. The beverage bar is open twenty-four hours with coffee, herbal teas, iced tea, and bottled water.

At Lake Austin Resort the health office is open daily with two registered nurses on staff. You will be sent a health questionnaire before arrival, and the resort requests you fill it in as completely as possible.

One of the best features of any spa is the massage. Lake Austin offers partial, full, and deep relaxation massages, and all are worth the extra cost. Your body will love you for it. Another wonderful spa feature is the facial. If you have missed this treat in your life, you owe it to your face to try it. Never has your skin felt so clean and glowing as after a facial.

Lectures on wide and varied topics are offered during the day, not just in the evenings. If you are a snorkeling addict, there may be a speech on "Safe Snorkeling," or for cooks, there's a walking tour of the herb and vegetable gardens with a special lecture on how to use herbs. And, if life has stretched you thin, hear "Dealing with Everyday Hassles."

Here in a beautiful setting, working with experts who care about your well-being, you will hate to leave. You'll just want to stay on forever being pampered and getting healthy. You'll leave knowing exactly why Lake Austin calls this week, "The Great Escape to Health and Fitness."

Out-of-the-Ordinary Retreats
Fifteen Texas Treasures

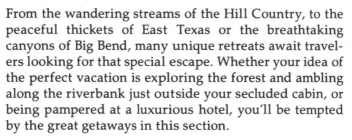

From the wandering streams of the Hill Country, to the peaceful thickets of East Texas or the breathtaking canyons of Big Bend, many unique retreats await travelers looking for that special escape. Whether your idea of the perfect vacation is exploring the forest and ambling along the riverbank just outside your secluded cabin, or being pampered at a luxurious hotel, you'll be tempted by the great getaways in this section.

What will it be? A rafting trip and gourmet feast on the Rio Grande? An African wildlife safari? A romantic dinner on a restored dining train? Whatever you're looking for, here's a collection of ideal retreats you won't find anywhere else.

CHAIN-O-LAKES

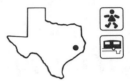

P.O. Box 218
Romayor 77368
713-592-2150

Hosts: Jimmy and Beverly Smith

Accommodations: Log cabins, rustic cabins, dormitories, campsites, screened cabanas, RV park, group facilities.

Rates: $ to $$

Location: 18 miles east of Cleveland between Highway 787 and 146 on Daniel Ranch Road.

Amenities: Conference center, rentals for pedal boats, boats, horseback rides, pony rides, carriage rides, fishing lakes, swimming lake, Rampage Water Coaster, snack bar, video games arcade, restaurant, club, gift shop, general store. Hunting leases and day hunting available nearby. No fishing licenses required.

Restrictions: No pets, no motorcycles, no motorized boats.

Chain-O-Lakes has been an East Texas playground since 1969, but old-timers may remember it as the Big Thicket Resort. Even before 1969, it was leased at various times to oil companies (as a sportsmen's retreat for their employees) and then to gravel companies for industrial use. The rustic cabins that are still standing were built during those years for the oil companies' outdoors lovers. And the gravel mining helped form some of the deep blue fishing lakes that fishermen love today.

The timber industry was in full swing too, and an old logging locomotive chugged in and never left. Although it is swampy and difficult to get to, feel free to explore this antique engine's rusting remains. Also, the road to the blueberry farm behind the resort was cleared to haul the massive pine logs to the sawmill.

In 1969, Jimmy's dad purchased the property and opened it as the Big Thicket Camp Park. Jimmy said, "The top attendance on any single weekend that first summer was 35 campers." Things have certainly changed since those early days—and all for the best! Chain-O-Lakes is now one of the best resorts in Texas and is still improving.

Cabin facilities vary from rustic to ritzy, and both feature kitchens, baths, air conditioning, and linens. If ritzy is for you, rent the new bed-and-breakfast log cabins. Fully equipped with wood-burning fireplaces, lofts, and antique furnishings, you even have a porch overlooking your own little lake. And, what would a porch be without a swing? So, swing your cares away at Chain-O-Lakes. You couldn't find a more perfect setting for a log cabin than among the dark green loblolly pines, sweetgums, Chinese tallows, and persimmons that rim the lakes. An occasional alligator glides by to remind you that he has priority billing in the lake.

Breakfast is eggs, bacon, and "the works" at the **Hilltop Country Inn**, and you can even reserve a horse-drawn carriage ride to breakfast. Better yet, you can arrange a moonlight champagne ride in this romantic 1833 carriage with a discreet never-opens-his-mouth driver. So, if you and your honey want to spoon under an East Texas moon, pop the cork and clink the glasses as you rock gently behind the dull clop of the horse's hooves.

Whatever you do, don't miss the Traditional Saturday Night Dinner at the inn. It boasts 5 courses over a 3-hour period. These marvelous recipes evolved from the old Hilltop Herb Farm that Madalene Hill began years ago west of Cleveland. The Smiths have moved her operation, lock, stock, and recipes, here to the Hilltop Country Inn.

Guests arrive at 6:00 P.M. for tours of the herb garden and gift shop, which includes tasting of wonderful concoctions such as 14-Karat Marmalade, Apple Rose Geranium Jelly, Hellfire and Damnation Jelly, and Tomato Chutney. All of these superb jams and jellies are offered for sale and make the perfect gift.

Seating for the first course is at 7:00, with the dessert arriving just before 10:00. As each course is presented, you are given a brief introduction into the ingredients of the recipe, particularly its seasonings and herbs. Your meal is accompanied by a complimentary serving of may wine, and begins with appetizers such as basil-dipped artichokes, ham and spinach pâté, and bleu cheese cake. You simply have to order a Hilltop Margarita. Jimmy and Beverly worked long and hard to create the perfect margarita, and they succeeded. They will even give you their recipe with the special ingredient—Hilltop Lime Tarragon Jelly.

Their soup is an excellent black bean with Hellfire, and a lettuce salad is served with the farm's classic herbal dressing. The entrée may be sole and salmon roulades with tarragon, and dessert a to-die-for Frangelico white chocolate mousse. You can see why reservations are required.

A gourmet brunch is served on Sunday, and here again, reservations are a must, for guests come from everywhere to be pampered with good food. In nice weather, move out to the patio that overlooks one of the lakes. The lord and master of this particular lake is a very large alligator affectionately called "The Governor." He's delighted to accept any tidbits you toss his way.

During the week, the Hilltop Inn offers a limited menu for room service. As you can expect, no matter what your choice is, it will be delicious, and much more fun than cooking.

If you are at Chain-O-Lakes in the summer, stroll down to the very back of the resort, and you'll see several acres of bushes. Here are some of the biggest, juiciest blueberries in Texas. Check with the owner; you can probably pick your own.

Right on the edge of Texas' mysterious Big Thicket, this wonderful resort covers about 300 acres of piney woods with 13 spring-fed lakes. The Big Thicket got its name from early Texas pioneers. This area was so dense with tangled growth that cutting a road through it was impossible. So the Big Thicket became a haven for outlaws and renegades. Pockets of this natural area still remain and are protected as a national preserve. The best way to explore this raw bit of nature is a canoe trip available from the **Big Thicket Museum** in nearby Saratoga.

If you have to bring the kids with you for a getaway or a longer stay, Chain-O-Lakes is a real winner. With so much to entertain all ages, you'll find plenty of time for just yourselves. Also, don't forget the off-season. Chain-O-Lakes is great even in the winter with those cozy fireplaces and plenty of trails for brisk hikes and jogging. Those horses want to be saddled up and hit the trails, too. In fact, the off-season may just be the best of times.

For an unforgettable wedding, consider Chain-O-Lakes. I got married on a beautiful day in April alongside one of the lakes. The white carriage picked us up and drove us to the wedding. A red carpet was rolled out, Pappy Selph played the Wedding March, and we had the most wonderful wedding in Texas. Chain-O-Lakes catered a fantastic meal, everyone danced in the Lodge, strolled around the lakes, sipped champagne under the trees, and we all had a glorious time. I couldn't have asked for a more perfect wedding, thanks to the wonderful people at Chain-O-Lakes.

As Jimmy puts it, "Our hope is that you will come to love our beautiful slice of nature as much as we do and continue to make your memories with us."

FOX FIRE

HCO1 Box 142
Vanderpool 78885
512-966-2200

Hosts: Wayne and Betty Boyce
Bill and Lanell Kellner

Accommodations: 6 cabins (one and two-bedroom)

Rates: $$ (Holiday rates higher)
Reservations strongly recommended.

Location: Highway 187 just north of Vanderpool and south of Lost Maples Natural Area.

Amenities: Pets and children welcome, fully equipped cabins, fireplaces, swimming, hiking, volleyball, badminton, horseshoes.

Restrictions: 2 nights minimum on weekends, no television, no telephones, no camping, no RVs, deposits required.

Fox Fire! The name captures your imagination immediately! And if you conjure up visions of wonderful log cabins on the banks of the Sabinal River in a remote section of the Hill Country, you will have accurately envisioned this perfect retreat.

You experience a feeling of isolation just getting to Fox Fire. Roads are free of billboards touting tourist attractions, and nothing blocks the scenery—not even the ranch gates. Any time of year is the perfect time to come to this area of Texas. In the fall, FM 470 and FM 337 have to be two of the most beautiful roads in Texas with flamboyant reds, yellows, and ambers in every hue. Call the **Lost Maples Natural Area** (512–966–3413) and find out when the bigtooth and canyon maples are at their peak. Here in this sheltered canyon is a touch of beauty right out of Vermont. The best time is usually November, but you can't always bet on Mother Nature to keep an exact schedule. Hiking into the canyon is a must, so bring those sturdy brogans and plenty of film.

Spring is wildflower time in the Hill Country. The rivers may be too cool for sinking into a tube and floating, but the weather is heavenly with brisk days and maybe-a-blanket nights. Summer is the time to hit the floats, drag out the picnic baskets, and hope you can get a reservation— anywhere. As for winter, it might just be the best of all. The crowds are gone, there's a definite snap in the air, and it's often downright cold at night. But at Fox Fire, you can build up a cozy fire, sip a glass of champagne, put a stuffed squab in the oven—and voila! The perfect getaway!

Every log cabin is air-conditioned and heated, and each comes with fully equipped kitchens with service for six. Not every cabin has a fireplace, so if it's fireplace weather, be sure to ask for one. No, you don't have to bring your own wood. But you do have to bring your own food because **Neal's** (Concan) is the nearest spot to eat, and you can't count on that being open in the winter. Gas and groceries are 2 miles down the road, but don't expect Kroger's.

The cabins are furnished in quaint antiques, and the sofa makes into a bed with all linens and towels included. All the comforts of home are here—from ceiling fans to ice makers—except telephones and television, but that's what you planned to leave behind. Of course you will find outside grills, comfortable lawn chairs, and a great view of the river, complete with its Fox Fire swimming hole. What a spot to get cabin fever.

Well, you say, that's all wonderful, but what is there to do? A lot of guests want to do nothing at all except maybe finish that book they started months ago or just sit and stare at the scenery and be glad there is a Fox Fire to enjoy. But, you can also go down the road a bit and rent a horse, hike all over the place, get up a volleyball game, toss a few horseshoes, or go birding. In the summer you can enjoy that cool lovely swimming hole or go over to **Garner State Park** and whoop it up with jillions of people. If gambling is in your blood, there's horseracing at Bandera Downs, and you can Texas two-step in Bandera, too. Special packages are available for hunters.

Fox Fire is definitely one of Texas' best "escapes," and as the brochure so truthfully points out, "You won't want to leave." Oh, for your trivia collection, fox fire is that phosphorescent light emitted from decaying timber and caused by fungi. It used to scare the daylights out of primitive people.

FRIO CANYON VACATIONLAND

Chamber of Commerce
P.O. Box 743
Leakey 78873
512-232-5222

Here in the beautiful Frio Canyon is the Country of 1,100 Springs. These massive springs flow together to make the Frio and Sabinal Rivers and create a nature's paradise on the far edge of the Texas Hill Country. A few evidences of civilization are found here and there, but the land is remarkably the same as when John Leakey found it in the 1850s.

Leakey (that's lake-ee), a Tennessean, brought his family to this untouched land and established a sawmill, using the cypress trees along the river for lumber and shingles. His town never made the big time for famous Texas towns, but the old Leakey Drug Store has sort of a claim to fame, and other historic buildings in Leakey still stand. At the drug store you can buy a soda from the ancient fountain and a T-shirt of more recent vintage.

Just west of Leakey, and a few miles north of Vanderpool, is the fabulous **Lost Maples State Natural Area**. In fall you may think of New England when it's time for the leaves to change, but here in a secluded little canyon you'll find the bigtooth maples, which are famous for their gorgeous fall color show. The park ranger recommends that you call in advance for the right time to see the trees at their loveliest (512–796–3771) because all sorts of weather factors can influence the color changes.

When Lost Maples does put on its extravaganza, the area is packed. Parking is at a premium, and you must hike into the canyon to see the trees at their best. So wear sturdy shoes, bring your camera, and call in advance.

Garner State Park is down from Leakey along the Frio River and is often referred to as the "park that has been loved to death." Reservations are a must, and no matter how early you call in advance, your chances are very slim of getting in (512–232–6132). It is nothing for the park to receive 4,000 phone calls a day. Built by the CCC boys in the 1930s during the Great Depression, Garner has 1½ miles of Frio River frontage, and every inch is filled with a park visitor floating, swimming, or just sitting on the bank.

Other than the river, the traditional Saturday night dances are the park's big draw. The juke box has every tune a teenage heart loves, and campers better be willing to listen to many selections played very loudly until late—very late. But, it's only on Saturday night. So, with the Frio, excellent camping facilities, wonderful scenery, and those Saturday night dances, no wonder poor old Garner State Park goes into shell shock after Labor Day.

But you have many other options for retreats other than Garner. There are **Neal's Lodges, Foxfire, Utopia on the River**, and about fifteen or so well-run tourist courts and camps along the Frio. Some have descriptions in this guidebook, and the Chamber has information on them all. Plus, if you want a secluded bed and breakfast cabin in the woods decorated with cute country decor, give the Garrisons a call at **Bluebird Hill** (512–966–3525). Bee is a professional story teller, and Roger is a professional artist. Your bed and breakfast cabin is set off by itself and your only company is the Hill Country's wildlife.

One of the most beautiful drives in Texas is FM 470 west from Bandera to Utopia. In the spring, the Hill Country stages its traditional riot of color with wildflowers, but it is absolutely magnificent in the fall when the trees get dressed in their autumn colors. It's hard to believe you are in the somewhat scruffy Hill Country of Texas and not in New England.

Tree lovers have to stop and visit with LeAnn Walker, who lives in a charming old house in Rio Frio. The live oak tree that covers her yard is unbelievable. Estimates go as high as 3,670 years old, the limbs branch out from the base to a point of 114 feet, *and it's still growing.* In 1990 the tree received a national award for being the largest live oak tree in the nation. Well, LeAnn loves her tree, but she is also a member of the **Rio Frio Bed-N-Breakfast Association**, which rents out second homes to people who want to see the Lost Maples, tube the Frio, or just enjoy a weekend in a special part of Texas. If you want a house to yourself, give LeAnn a call at 512–232–6633. Not only will she arrange a fabulous weekend getaway, she'll show you her prize live oak.

For those who like ruins, ask at Garner State Park about the site of **Mission Nuestra Senora de la Candelaria del Canon** founded in 1762, the **Texas Rangers' Camp Sabinal** established in 1856, and **Fort Inge** established in 1849.

The *Uvalde Leader-News* publishes the *Southwest Texas Visitors' Guide* every year, and it is excellent. Send $1.35 for postage to Box 740, Uvalde 78802, and request the guide.

Of all the enchanting parts of the Hill Country, the Frio Canyon is the most wonderful of them all. Let's hope "progress" never passes its way.

THE FOOTHILLS SAFARI CAMP AT FOSSIL RIM

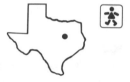

P.O. Drawer 329
Glen Rose 76043
817-897-3398

Accommodations: 6 private luxury tents, each sleeps 2 people.

Rates: $$$

Location: Take US 67 southwest out of Glen Rose for 3 miles and turn left at the sign.

Amenities: Safaris last 3 days and 2 nights, longer safaris available, audio-visual equipment, wildlife library, gourmet meals, tents with central heat and air conditioning plus private bath, lodge, bar, hiking, fossil hunting, gift shop. A list of what to bring is sent to you in advance.

Restrictions: No pets, children 18 and under are welcome only on preplanned family safaris, no alcohol may be carried in, and alcoholic drinks are extra.

Have you ever longed to go on a camera safari to the wilds of darkest Africa where herds of exotic animals roam the veldt? Well, pack up your bush jacket and pith helmet and head for Fossil Rim, one of the world's best animal parks. If you could replace the oaks with acacia trees and add Mt. Kenya, you would find Africa right here in Texas because Fossil Rim's 2,900 acres of valleys, vistas, and savannahs are home to 1,000 endangered animals.

Fossil Rim is a wildlife conservation organization fully accredited by the prestigious American Association of Zoological Parks and Aquariums Species Survival Plan. Fossil Rim's Species Survival Plan includes the cheetah, red wolf, white rhinoceros, Grevy's zebra, scimitar-horned oryx, and addax. On your safari you will be treated to a close-up view of these animals while learning more about them and the threat of extinction.

Your safari begins with a late afternoon cocktail party in the lodge complemented by a sunset that Fossil Rim has ordered just for you. After a briefing on all the events that await you, a gourmet dinner is served. The Fossil Rim Safari Camp has its own chef, so be prepared for a very filling stay. After dinner you can watch television or a movie, but the best show is on the verandah through the telescope. In the clear country air, the stars shine just for your viewing.

Your tent quarters will be small, but very comfortable. The bathroom will be a pleasant surprise with its shower and modern facilities. With any luck, you won't need the heat or air conditioning and will be able to leave your windows open so you can experience the thrill of hearing the red wolves' mournful howling. Some nights these rare creatures will sing for hours—even when there isn't a full moon. The ordinary visitor to Fossil Rim doesn't get to see the red wolves because they are being prepared to return to the wild and must be kept from human contact. Safari guests are allowed to visit their pens, but the wolves are shy and hide in the brush most of the day. The newest addition to the Species Survival Plan at Fossil Rim is the rare and endangered Mexican wolf.

Your second day will be busy, busy, busy. After watching the sunrise from the porch of your tent, the animals arrive at the watering hole for their morning drink. A monster breakfast is served, and then it's time to visit the red wolf and cheetah facilities. The cheetah program began in 1984 and today nearly twenty percent of all the cheetahs in the United States can trace their origins back to Fossil Rim. As few as 5,000 of these magnificent cats remain in the wild and less than 200 are in American zoos. Large spacious pens allow these animals, considered to be the fastest on earth, to run at top speed. But Fossil Rim's cheetahs are like wild cheetahs; they love to loll about in the shade, cleaning their coats and nuzzling the kittens.

You then have some free time to birdwatch or hunt fossils before another superb meal. The afternoon is filled with a game drive and visit to the rhinoceros house. All rhinoceroses are a dirty gray, but the white rhino has wide square lips. Both species have been slaughtered, almost to the point of extinction, for their "horns." Although the rhinoceros' "horn" is just matted hair, it is believed to be an aphrodisiac.

Rhinoceroses have a reputation for meanness, but that is not an accurate reflection of their disposition. Actually, these big ugly critters are very fond of being patted and scratched and enjoy human attention. And at Fossil Rim you can stroke that tough hide without endangering yourself at all.

The group passes around a camera that takes slides and each person shoots photos as the drive progresses (in addition to the photos that guests are taking with their cameras).

After dinner the group views them and votes are taken on the best shot. The winner is awarded a bottle of champagne. None of the photos may be *National Geographic* quality, but it's still a delightful evening.

After another wonderful dinner, it's back to the telescope, wolf howls, and, most likely, an early bedtime. On your drives at Fossil Rim you will see silly ostriches demanding handouts, the sleek sable antelope, gemsbok, gigantic European red deer, greater kudu, waterbuck, blackbuck from India, Grant's zebra, axis deer, blesbok, fallow deer, Grant's gazelle, springbok, sika deer, shaggy wildebeest, aoudad sheep, llamas, and wildlife native to Texas. Flocks of wild turkeys spread their tailfeathers for a show, and whitetail deer leap gracefully back into the brush. A dead tree is home for more than fifty turkey buzzards.

Your last day begins with a drive to the giraffe compound. Did you know that the giraffe is the only animal that can distinguish colors? Did you know that when baby giraffes are born, they fall six feet and land standing up? These gentle giants are quite docile and will probably approach your vehicle. Next you'll head up to the overlook to enjoy a spectacular view of the preserve and explore the gift shop. Here you'll find world-class souvenirs, books, gifts, rocks and minerals, and many other treasures.

At brunch you'll enjoy your final gourmet meal. Then you'll have to say goodby to the talented and knowledgeable people that made your safari so perfect. But you will leave respecting their work and promising to return to hear the red wolves.

LAJITAS

Star Route 70, Box 400
Terlingua 79852
915-424-3471
(reservations, in Texas: 800-527-4078)

Accommodations: Badlands Hotel, La Cuesta Motel, Officer's Quarters Hotel, The Cavalry Post Motel, and a few condominiums.

Rates: $$

Location: At the very western tip of Big Bend National Park on Highway 170.

Amenities: Horseback riding, tennis, swimming pool, golf, bicycle rentals, bingo, dancing, hiking, rafting.

Once upon a time, not so very long ago, the only building in Lajitas (Little Rocks) was the Lajitas Trading Post. This small adobe building with a single antique gas pump looked like a setting for a Pancho Villa movie. Cold beer attracted a clientele that could use a good scrubbing and a shave. Here was the ultimate outpost of civilization.

Today, the Trading Post still sells cold beer, but now its clientele wears designer jeans and George Strait hats. Progress has come to Lajitas. Fortunately, progress didn't halt Clay Henry's drinking ability. Clay Henry is the Trading Post's beer-guzzling goat. This talented critter can clamp a beer bottle between those rubbery lips, toss back those horns, and chug-a-lug the drink in a matter of seconds. Clay Henry really isn't picky about his brand, but most tourists buy him a Lone Star, or several Lone Stars.

The Mischer Corporation of Houston has purchased just about everything in and around Lajitas and is creating a

Palm Springs in Texas. The climate is perfect for that scene but, so far, no big-name movie stars have bought homes here. And Lajitas has managed to retain its air of remoteness. Just pray that the ultimate in civilization doesn't arrive—the shopping mall.

Main Street Lajitas is still the only attraction. There's only one restaurant, one liquor store, one drug store, and (so far) only one gift shop selling T-shirts. The newest hotel, **The Officer's Quarters**, overlooks the golf course, and **The Badlands Hotel** is upstairs over the bar. You will be closer to the swimming pool and tennis courts at **La Cuesta** and **The Cavalry Post**. All look mighty good after you've been out on the desert.

Summer days can be grueling in the desert, but the nights are cool and delightful. And Lajitas' weather is perfect both day *and* night from October through April. The sky is always its beautiful blue, temperatures are not screaming off the top of the thermometers, and the desert is absolutely gorgeous.

Plan your days to include an overnight raft trip down the Rio Grande with **Far Flung Adventures**. Here is a Texas highlight that everyone should do. Reservations are necessary, so call 915–371–2489. Far Flung's office is over at Terlingua, an old mercury mining town that you will want to explore. For years, Terlingua's only inhabitants were ghosts, but now real live people are moving in and Terlingua is losing its ghost town status.

The **Lajitas Museum and Desert Garden** capture the magic of Big Bend. Begin your Lajitas getaway here, where you get a wonderful overview of the area's history and flora and fauna.

You may not be heading west to go home, but make a detour and drive the historic **River Road**, voted one of the ten best roads in the United States. Highway 170 to Presidio follows the winding course of the Rio Grande. It was in this remote area that bandits, bootleggers, revolutionaries, Comanches, and even a few good guys like "Black Jack" Pershing made their mark.

Pershing and his Negro troops spent fruitless months searching for the elusive Pancho Villa in these endless canyons. Then when prohibition took effect, the bootleggers made their fortunes smuggling booze into a thirsty Texas, and Lajitas was a favorite crossing site. In fact, the Cavalry Post is located on the site of one of Pershing's camps.

Just before your road ends, stop and visit **Fort Leaton**, which was a private fort. The story goes that Leaton got tired of the thieving Indians that hung out around his fort, so he invited them in for a feast. After lots of food and even more whiskey the doors of the fort were locked and Leaton had his men shoot and kill every Indian. This effectively stopped the stealing at Fort Leaton.

The scenery is spectacular along the River Road, and in the spring when the flaming red ocotilla blooms, it is even more gorgeous. Here you can truly get away from it all. For motorcycle riders, the River Road is cycling at its very best. A roadside park with brightly colored replicas of tepees makes a perfect spot for a picnic break.

Lajitas, like Big Bend, is a hiker's paradise. There are plenty of options for half- or full-day hiking and backcountry trips. Geology lovers will find geometrical basalt formations, petrified forests, and unusual canyons. Pools and springs flow out of the cracked earth, and wild burros and coyotes lurk in the underbrush with old sneaky snakes, so don't forget your boots.

Tours are even available that continue on to Copper Canyon in old Mexico. Call the 800 number for more information.

For those who love spectacular mountains, vast deserts, rich history, a sense of adventure, and an alcoholic goat, Lajitas is perfect.

NEAL'S

Box 165
Concan 78838
512-232-6118

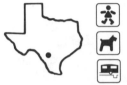

Hosts: Mary Anna Buchanan Roosa and John S. Graves, Jr.

Accommodations: 60 cabins, 10 RV sites, 25 campsites.

Rates: $ to $$

Location: One mile east of the intersection of U.S. 83 and Highway 127, 20 miles north of Uvalde.

Amenities: Swimming, floating, fishing, birdwatching, hiking, horseback riding, hayrides, grocery store, and restaurant.

Restrictions: Use only wood and charcoal available at store. No firearms, no motorcycles, no jumping from rocks or trees, pets must be on a leash, no fireworks. Reservations are taken for cabins and hookups only, not for campsites. Reservations for each year begin on January 1. During June, July, and August a three night minimum is required. Dates vary in the winter and off-season and so do rates. Check for dates before you go. Restaurant hours vary, too.

If you're talking about special places in Texas, Neal's has to come to mind. More than fifty years ago Tom Neal built a few cabins in the canyon of the Frio River. He intended for them to be used by hunters, but word about the beauty of the canyon got around and more cabins went up. Then Tom's daughter, Mary Tom Buchanan, and her husband, John, transformed Neal's from a hunter's camp into a vacationer's camp by adding more cabins, RV sites, and camping areas. Next came a country store, a post office, and a restaurant. The reservations poured in. The ads read, "In the cedar belt of the cool West Texas Hills on the beautiful Frio River, 285 miles from Houston, 2,000 feet above sea level, all buildings of native rock and cedar, electric lights, showers, and sanitary sewage." Neal's was a total success.

The Buchanans retired in 1983 and sold the resort, but the Frio was in their blood and they bought it back. Now Tom Neal's grandchildren, Mary Anna Buchanan Roosa and John S. Graves, Jr., and their spouses run the resort. Chances are you'll talk to Mary Anna when you call. All agree that Neal's should be left as it was in the 1930s.

Most cabins have kitchenettes and the store stocks a variety of staples. However, you'll have to bring any special foods you may want. Pillows and bed linens are furnished, but *not* towels. Neal's also doesn't furnish kitchen utensils or dishes. You can rent towels, but don't forget those pots and pans.

Once you spy those old wooden and stone cottages blending into the land and trees you might call them "rustic" or "basic," but they aren't primitive. You can request one with air conditioning. And, if you didn't come on your vacation to cook, **Neal's Cafe** is just across the road! The crowds aren't there just because it's one of the very few restaurants for a number of miles. They know where to find plenty of good food and low checks. The chicken fried steak is to die for. Breakfast is fluffy pancakes and sausage or fried eggs just the way you like them.

But, the main attraction of Neal's is the Frio. As every beginning Spanish student knows, *frio* is the Spanish word for cold, very cold. On a blistering Texas summer day, the Frio is the place. At the swimming hole, relax on an inner tube, snorkel in the clean green water, swim a few strokes, take a few dives off the diving board, or try to catch an elusive Frio fish. Life at Neal's revolves around the Frio River, or there probably wouldn't be a Neal's.

Floating connoisseurs believe the Frio is the best river in Texas. The scenery is gorgeous as you drift past hidden glens where white-tailed deer hide and wild turkeys strut their stuff. Nowhere will you see a sign advertising anything. The river is totally pristine and uncluttered; it's nice to know a beer joint or the golden arches isn't just around the bend.

You can also enjoy a scenic horseback ride or a hike on trails that wind through thick brush, overhanging cypress trees, clusters of live oaks, fields of wildflowers, and a myriad of bird songs.

The Audubon Society rates Concan as one of the best bird watching sites in the country. So don't be surprised if you see some guests just sitting quietly and patiently waiting for any of more than 100 species of birds to make an appearance.

You'll love Neal's if you love the Hill Country and nature. But don't expect the Hyatt Regency or even the Holiday Inn. Neal's is totally different, yet so totally special that it's no wonder that no one wants anything changed.

FLAGSHIP HOTEL

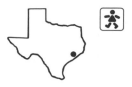

25th and Seawall Boulevard
Galveston 77550
800-392-6542 (Texas)
409-762-9000

Accommodations: 518 rooms.

Rates: $$ to $$$

Location: Take I-45 south to Houston to 25th Street.
Turn right and drive straight to the Flagship.

Amenities: Pool, spa, restaurant, lounge.

Strolling along Galveston's Seawall, as its massive hunks of
granite break the pounding surf, it is hard to believe that
after the dreadful events of September 8, 1900, all that
remained of the city was death and destruction. The Great
Storm had practically leveled Galveston. But the city fought
back against relentless, unpredictable storms and built its
famous Seawall out of thousands of tons of Texas granite.
Today visitors rarely note this impressive engineering feat.

Galveston slowly recovered from the devastation, and now
it is one of the most popular resort towns on the Gulf Coast.
What would a resort town be without a pleasure pier?
Galveston began its 1,000-foot pier as far back as 1912,
only a few years after The Great Storm. The idea was there,
but it was 1931 before construction got underway. World
War II caused a serious delay, but by 1944 the 4-block long
pier, off of 25th Street, was a reality.

With its crowded T-head fishing pier and Coney Island fla-
vor, even the local citizenry found their pleasure pier to be a
favorite spot. Then, in 1965, came the crowning touch—the
luxurious Flagship Hotel . . . America's first and only
hotel built entirely over the water.

For years the Flagship was the crème de la crème of Galveston's hostelries. How romantic it was to sit in the bar's big comfy chairs on a wild, stormy afternoon watching the ocean give the Seawall a cruel lashing. You could sit sipping drinks for hours, mesmerized by the sea.

Then hard times fell on the Flagship. Rooms became seedy, as did the bar and dining room. The poor old Flagship was no longer the vogue place to stay. Galveston was growing rapidly, and newer hotels and condos seduced the Flagship's clientele.

Fortunately, in 1988 refurbishing of the hotel was begun. Now the ambiance of the Flagship is fresh, new, and exciting with its bright art deco calypso colors. She has the feel of a luxury liner, and you almost expect the registration desk clerk to say, "Welcome aboard. We sail at midnight."

If fishing is your sport, try your luck on the pier's T-head. The hotel will be glad to equip you with fishing gear and supply the day's weather report. You can join the energetic roller skaters or take leisurely surrey rides on the Seawall, but most of the crowd meanders along enjoying the sea air and sunshine or browsing in the shell shops for seaside souvenirs.

You won't find a beach along most of the Seawall, so you'll have to go down to the old faithful **Stewart's Beach** or **West Beach** to feel that squishy wet sand between your toes.

The Flagship's spacious rooms carry out the calypso color scheme of bright orange and sea green, and all overlook the ocean. As you sit on your balcony, you can't help but feel you're cruising the Gulf of Mexico. You are not just looking at the ocean from a hotel on the beach—you are looking at the ocean from above those whitecaps. No other hotel can offer this very special experience but the Flagship. No matter how often you return to this unique hotel, the charm remains.

Now you can hop the rail to Galveston on the **Texas Limited**. This string of restored rail cars makes a 2½ hour run from Thursday through Sunday. The scenery may not be Copper Canyon or castles in Spain, but it's fun to get away from the frantic freeway for a change. Make your reservation with Ticketron (713–526–1709). You can really make the most of your weekend and board one of the two gambling ships that cruise out into the gulf. The Galveston Visitors Bureau is just down the street from the Flagship at 2106 Seawall Boulevard. Stop by and get a stack of brochures on Galveston's many tourist attractions. Or, before you go, give them a call at 409–763–4311.

THE ADOLPHUS PENTHOUSE

1321 Commerce St.
Dallas 75202
214-742-8200
800-221-9083

Accommodations: 5-room penthouse.

Rates: $$$$

Amenities: Private elevator, great view.

Have you ever wanted a very special place in the middle of a high-stepping city where you can get away from it all without being too far away from the bright lights and the action? The fabulous old Adolphus has the perfect retreat for you with its breathtakingly elegant penthouse. When you get off the elevator and take the short flight of stairs into this magnificent hideaway, you enter a world all your own. You feel like you are a zillion miles from the fast lane, and in a way, you really are. Here atop one of the most prestigious hotels in the United States you have the ultimate in a great getaway.

To describe the Adolphus penthouse, you have to conjure up all of the superlatives. The exquisite parlor is gorgeous with its overstuffed sofa and chairs, handsome oriental rugs, priceless antiques, and even a baby grand piano. The piano should come in handy for easy listening music during the intimate gourmet dinners that the Adolphus chef will prepare for you to serve in the formal dining room. Or perhaps you may plan a small elegant cocktail party with the piano music creating the perfect effect. You will find the bar stocked with setups, wine, champagne, and liquor of your choice.

Down the hall is the huge bedroom with its warm, inviting, four-poster canopy bed. This Paul Bunyan bed is so high off the floor you need the steps to climb in and literally snuggle down into the lap of luxury. A seating area and hidden television add to the bedroom's romantic decor.

Completing your metropolitan hideaway is a bath and dressing room with all of the amenities for a luxurious hot bath. But, before you lock your penthouse door, take a tour of the hotel lobby. Its antiques and *objects d'art* are equal to masterpieces found in the Louvre in Paris, the Metropolitan Museum in New York, and in the great estates of Europe. A little booklet called "Treasures of the Adolphus" makes a handy guide to the incredible are found in this fabulous hotel.

This wonderful hotel was built in 1912, and all of this opulence and tradition began with a lowly bottle of beer. Adolphus Busch was so successful with his beer in Texas, he decided to repay Dallas with a showplace of splendor. The result was 21 stories of red brick and gray granite adorned with ornate figures out of Greek mythology and capped with a tower in the shape of a beer bottle. One of the two chandeliers Busch had commissioned in 1904 for the World's Fair in St. Louis is now hanging over the escalator.

Should you decide to dine out, all you have to do is make a reservation for the world-acclaimed **French Room**. May we recommend the Beluga caviar, royal squab with truffles, and lobster sausage with sea urchins? Or should you prefer the privacy of the penthouse for dinner, do go down to the lobby museum for tea. Choose from a collection of teas, ports, sherries, or exotic coffees (from all over the world) to sip while you enjoy the dainty finger sandwiches and petit fours.

Everybody that is anybody stays at the Adolphus, and your penthouse may just have been the rooms of William Jennings Bryan, Charles Lindbergh, all the U.S. presidents, the brightest of the movie stars, and all the Texas-Oklahoma alumni during their annual pigskin contest. Queen Elizabeth and Prince Phillip stayed at the Adolphus on their recent tour, but requested the 2-bedroom suite, rather than the one-bedroom penthouse. The 2-bedroom suite is actually a bit less expensive.

Dallas has many impressive sights, excellent museums, and fine restaurants, but you can have the best of them all right here at the Adolphus. Plus, you'll have your own private world in the penthouse.

VANISHING TEXAS RIVER CRUISE

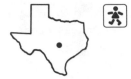

P.O. Box 901
Burnet 78611
512-756-6986

Rates: $$

Location: From Burnet, drive 3 miles west on Highway 29 to RM 2341. Turn north on RM 2341 and continue 13.5 miles to entrance.

Schedule Time: 2¹/₂ hour nature trip, first cruise departs 11 A.M. Bald Eagle season is November through March. Wildflower and spring migratory bird season is April and May. Sunset and dinner cruise season is May through October.

Amenities: Open year-round, food service, restrooms, enclosed seating, gift shop, group rates, charters.

Restrictions: Reservations highly recommended, no pets.

Have you ever just wanted to take a cruise to nowhere? No billboards touting real estate, no Golden Arches, no shopping sprees, no hikes up scenic peaks to tempt you? Well, you can simply sit and watch the river flow by on the Vanishing Texas River Cruise (VTRC). But your curiosity will probably get the best of you and you'll pull out the binoculars like the rest of the passengers and join in the thrill of spotting the elusive wildlife hidden among the dense brush of the river's banks.

At certain times of the year you'll want to tilt your lens skyward instead of toward the banks. If you're lucky you might spy the great American Bald Eagle soaring around his winter nesting grounds. The eagles on Lake Buchanan comprise one of the largest eagle groups in Texas and usually number between eighteen and thirty-five birds. Their winter season in Texas is from November to March, so make your reservations for this time of year as soon as possible.

All of this relaxation and scenery began in 1982 when Llano County rancher Ed Low wanted to share this unspoiled area in Texas. He put together his first cruise in an open-air boat, and one day the tour spotted an eagle. Then they began to see eagles all the time. Finally Ed got a fully climate-controlled boat and passengers quit freezing as they watched for these magnificent, endangered birds. Eagles seem to be more active on cold cloudy days, so be prepared to juggle camera, gloves, binoculars, and bird books when you spot an amazing wing spread.

You'll see our national bird gliding effortlessly overhead with his eagle eye searching mercilessly for fish. As everyone knows, the bald eagle is not bald. From a distance, his snow-white head feathers give him a bald appearance. It's difficult to get a close-up photo, since eagles are not fond of people. But your expert guide will make sure you don't miss any sightings—in the air or on the ground.

You may be most interested in seeing eagles, but all year long you can see other birds flying over Lake Buchanan on their way north or south. Pelicans, gulls, cormorants, and ring-billed gulls thrive on inland lakes.

If all this bird watching makes you hungry, the boat serves hot coffee, fresh sandwiches, homemade soup, and soft drinks. Or you can bring your own lunch.

You'll also pass by the **Fall Creek Vineyards** owned by Ed and Susan Auler. Fall Creek has won many awards and produces excellent chenin blanc, emerald riesling, and French colombard. Their elegant tasting room and visitors center is open for guests on the last Saturday of each month.

VTRC offers all sorts of packages for dinner cruises, vineyard cruises, and hydro-jet rides to **Colorado Bend State Park** for a picnic, hike, or swim.

Several places in the area are great for an overnight visit. Ed Low's bed and breakfast near VTRC has a bubbling fountain and a swimming pool right at your front door. Ed also runs VTRC, so you can make reservations at his bed and breakfast by calling the phone number listed for the river cruise. The big Hill Country moon rises over the lake, and the stars were never brighter. Quarters are 2 bedrooms, each with private bath, and Ed serves a hearty breakfast of eggs, ham, and hot biscuits. You can get a super package deal that includes this overnight stay.

Down the road in Llano, the historic **Badu House** offers 8 guest rooms furnished with turn-of-the-century antiques, excellent meals, and the Llanite Bar. Call 915–247–4304.

The same good folks that run VTRC are now offering another cruise, called the Lake Marble Falls Cruise, which is hosted aboard the *General Johnson.* On this scenic tour, you enjoy a taped narration on the historic Colorado River and scenic Marble Falls. Looking down onto Lake Travis from the Max Starke Dam on Lake Marble Falls is a big highlight on this 1½ hour tour. Gourmet dinner cruises are offered on the weekend and a luncheon cruise is offered on Sunday. They run tours all year, and you can reach them at VTRC or at Lake Marble Falls Cruise, 307 Buena Vista, Marble Falls, 78654. Cruises depart from Lakeside Park and reservations are required. You can book your reservations by calling 512-693-6126.

Texas' Highland Lakes area has many star attractions, so plan for a fun-filled getaway with lots to see and do. For all the details, call 512–793–6666.

TEXAN DINING TRAIN

Southern Pacific Amtrak Station
1000 N. Alamo
San Antonio 78215
512-225-7245

Rates: $$$

Time Schedule: 7 P.M. Wednesday through Saturday.
5 P.M. Sunday.
Boarding begins 1 hour before departure.

Amenities: Group rates, private parties, special trains.

Restrictions: No children under 14, 7-day advance cancellation for refund, gentlemen must wear jackets, gratuities not included.

> "Gonna take a sentimental journey,
> Gonna stir up memories.
> Gonna take a sentimental journey,
> Gonna set my heart at ease."
> **Johnny Mercer**

Before the advent of jet engines and metal detectors, the *only* way to travel was by train. During the 1930s, '40s, and '50s, the great passenger trains were romanticized in fiction and song. Everyone knew the names of tunes like "City of New Orleans," "Super Chief," "20th Century Limited," and the thrill of hearing the conductor call, "All aboard!" But the big jets effectively wiped out passenger trains just as the steam engine had made the stagecoach obsolete.

But now, on the Texan Dining Train, you can once again take a sentimental journey on the grand old cars of past eras. Relive the days of luxurious dining cars, impeccable service, and gourmet foods and fine wines as you roar toward a Texas sunset of fiery pinks, exotic purples, and brilliant golds.

The Texan is totally authentic. These opulent cars have been meticulously restored to their original magnificence. The art deco decor and the sleek stainless steel trim typify the era when train travel was in all its glory.

The General Motors engines were built between 1950 and 1953 and can travel up to 65 miles per hour and generate 1,750 horsepower each. As the train glides along the tracks west of San Antonio to Hondo, passengers rock gently in the elegant 1948 "California Zephyr" car while sipping cocktails and watching the sun's evening farewell. But, don't miss a tour of all the other restored cars.

The "California Zephyr" has been converted into a dome dining car and is one of the most popular cars on the train. "The Nambe" is the oldest car on The Texan. Dating back to 1937, the car was furnished with a plush bar, a barber shop, a shower for passengers, and staff quarters for twelve. Named after a Navajo Indian pueblo, "The Nambe" had enjoyed its glamorous career as a catfish restaurant before its restoration. A photograph of the painting of the pueblo hangs in place of the original.

The Santa Fe re-equipped "The Super Chief" in 1950 and the Santa Fe 500 was designed to have a complete bar under the dome, as well as a splendid dining area called The Turquoise Room. It was built to accommodate movie stars as they traveled from Los Angeles to Chicago.

The round trip takes $3^1/2$ hours and travels through the heart of South Texas ranch country on one of the high-speed main lines of the Southern Pacific Railroad. As a result, you may see piggyback and freight trains zooming by your window. Southern Pacific also supplies the crew, which consists of a conductor, engineer, and brakeman. The conductor is the only one in America permanently assigned to a dining car. The rest of the 27-member staff works to make your trip a truly memorable experience—they do an excellent job.

After cocktails and imaginatively delectable hors d'oeuvres, the maître d' escorts you to your dining car for a tasty start on a four-course feast. Savor the soup duJour and Caesar salad, and choose fish, chicken, or chateaubriand for your entree, and finish up with an elegant dessert. The wine list is excellent but all alcoholic drinks are extra.

As Johnny Mercer sang in "Sentimental Journey," "Seven, that's the time I leave for heaven." So, be at San Antonio's Amtrak Station before 7 P.M. to embark on your own sentimental journey.

COWBOY MORNING

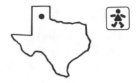

Figure 3 Ranch
Rt.1 Box 69
Claude 79019-9712
806-944-5562
800-658-2613

Hosts: Tom and Anne Christian

Rates: $

Time Schedule: Departs ranch at 7:30 A.M. May through September. (By reservation only.)

Location: Directions furnished.

Back in the days of the rough and tough cattle drives, a hard-riding cowpoke only earned about a dollar a day, and the occupational hazards included marauding Indians, stampedes, and rain, sand, hail, and dust storms. Each hand's meals were furnished, allowing him all the beans, sourdough biscuits, and coffee he wanted—if the chuck wagon wasn't low on supplies. When you stop and think about it, the American cowboy is the only laboring man in history that became a folk hero.

Of course cowboys still ride the range, but their salaries have increased tremendously—even at minimum wage. Camp fare has undergone a definite improvement, too. Beans and sourdough biscuits are still on the menu, but they have been enhanced with scrambled eggs, bacon, sausage, pancakes, and orange juice. So, when you head 'em up and move 'em out for the Figure 3 Ranch, be prepared for a feast as big as the outdoors.

When you arrive at the Figure 3 Ranch you will be visiting a working cattle ranch that has been operating since 1903. Great-grandfather George Christian came to Texas shortly after the Civil War, and in 1889 son Jim Christian and another brother came to the Panhandle to work for the fabled JA Ranch. When the JA allowed cowboys to buy parcels of the ranch land, Jim Christian established his own ranch, the Figure 3. The ranch is now owned by Tom Christian and his wife, Anne, and when they aren't cooking and hosting a Cowboy Morning, they are hard at work running the ranch.

Mule-drawn wagons wait for you at the gate and carry you across this historic 7,000-acre ranch. All sorts of prairie birds take flight as you traverse the grasslands, and infinite varieties of wild flowers add to the beauty of the landscape. Suddenly, out of nowhere, you see the Grand Canyon of Texas—Palo Duro Canyon—and the campsite for your memorable "Taste of the Old West" is right on the edge of this spectacular cleft in the flat treeless landscape.

Palo Duro was carved with the help of relentless wind and rain over the course of millions of years. This 120-mile-long, 1,000-foot-chasm displays more than 90 million years of geologic time in its bands of beautiful ochre, red, and magenta. Indians camped in this protected canyon for centuries. But it got its name from Coronado who called it *Palo Duro*, or "hard wood," because of its tough juniper trees. In 1874, Col. Ranald Mackenzie defeated the Comanches who had settled in Palo Duro, and the ranchers moved in.

You won't have time to hike the canyon today, because the sweet aroma of mesquite wood pulls you back from the canyon's rim to manhole-cover-size skillets filled with fluffy scrambled eggs and sizzling sausage. On the side, two gallons of coffee steeps in a gigantic enamel coffee pot. Here you'll find coffee that will test your constitution. The grounds are thrown in on top of the water, and as the coffee boils, the grounds sink to the bottom. Heavy Dutch ovens are filled with sourdough biscuits, and, believe me, just the biscuits alone are worth the trip. Cook James Robinson shares the following recipe for these heavenly morsels:

Use a spider bottom Dutch oven. Set it on hot coals and put coals on top of lid. Then you mix up:

1/2 gal. sourdough starter
10 lbs. flour
1 cup shortening
1 cup sugar
1 Palmful of baking powder
2 pinches baking soda

Depending on the wind, you should have about 600 biscuits in fifteen minutes. Then add cream gravy and ah-h-h-h-h-h! But everything tastes so good in the open air under a Texas sun with a breeze stirring the tall grass.

Your cooks are actually ranch hands, and when you climb aboard the wagon to leave this delightful adventure, they pack up and return to their ranching duties. But before you go you are treated to lessons in lassoing, rope twirling, and even cow chip tossing. (Not to worry, these are old *dried* cow chips.) However, many of the guests wander back to the canyon's rim to enjoy its beauty as long as possible. Why not reserve a place for the Figure 3's Evening Dinner? You can come back and enjoy a Palo Duro sunset and steaks or hamburgers as only Figure 3 can cook them.

To fully experience Palo Duro, you must also visit **Palo Duro Canyon State Park** and see "Texas," a musical that tells the history of the legendary canyon. (The production runs from mid-June to the end of August.) In fact, whether you plan to stay a day or a week, just settle back and let the Amarillo Convention and Visitor Council plan a full itinerary for you. Their "Day in the Old West" is a real winner. Just dial 1–800–692–1338, polish up your boots, pull on your jeans, and get set for a rootin', tootin' Texas good time.

YACHT-O-FUN

2216 Windsor Dr.
Richardson 75082
214-238-8224
903-786-2966 (Boat docked at Loe's
Highport Marina, near Pottsboro)

Hosts: Buddy and Diana Greer

Accommodations: 2 staterooms, 2 baths.

Location: 4 miles north of Pottsboro. The Greer's will send a detailed map with your reservation confirmation.

Rates: $$$

Amenities: Special honeymoon cruises, moonlight cruises, day-long charters.

Restrictions: No children, no pets, bring your own alcoholic beverages, smoking permitted in designated areas.

Yachting, anyone? No, it's not the *QE-2*, but it's a lot cozier, and you can dine at the captain's table every night without dressing for dinner. Although the *QE-2* certainly offers gourmet fare, so does *Yacht-O-Fun.* You know it's good because the captain cooks it himself—with some valuable assistance from the first mate.

This Bluewater Coastal Cruiser is fifty-one feet long with two staterooms, one with a full bath and queen-size bed. Diana and her friends quilted the elegant cover. The smaller bedroom is just big enough for its three-quarter-size bed and the bath comes with a hand-held shower head. When two couples go yachting, the captain and his mate sleep on the couch in the stateroom.

Separating these elegant quarters is the large stateroom and a full galley with a dining area. And if you're interested,

Buddy is delighted to show off a monster 350-horsepower engine that is built to cruise.

After you stow your gear and relax on the sofa, violin music will come wafting through the air as Diana starts to make you feel comfortable. After casually heading off to nowhere in particular, Captain Buddy cuts the motor, and beaches the boat on a red sandy spit. You gently rock beneath the darkening sky and notice that the stars at night really are big and bright even on the northern edge of Texas. As you watch them sparkle brilliantly, all troubles drift away.

Although the Yacht-O-Fun is a floating bed and breakfast, the Greer's will be happy to create a mouth-watering dinner, at an added cost, when both sets of guests make a special request to dine under the stars. If you decide to dine on board, you'll enjoy a quiet, romantic meal. Even though you'll be old friends with the captain and mate in a matter of minutes, if you and your companion prefer to dine *tete-a-tete*, that's perfectly agreeable with the crew. They know when to disappear.

Getting on toward midnight the captain starts the engines and heads toward the dock. You may have envisioned a restorative sleep while floating weightlessly on the lake, but early morning fishermen and water skiers have no sense of romance, and you are apt to be rudely awakened with motors whizzing by. Instead, the aroma of coffee wakes you to a wonderful day on the lake.

You'll probably want to linger over the fresh fruit and orange juice a long time, but remember, you have lots of lake to explore. Lake Texoma has jillions of coves and islands, all beckoning you for a morning swim. On the stern, right above water level, is a platform with a ladder. Buddy recommends diving off the platform and floating around lazily.

In what seems like minutes, Diana will have one of her

bountiful brunches ready. Stuff yourself with homemade hashbrowns, fresh cantaloupe, French toast, bacon, eggs, and coffee. After brunch while docked on one of Lake Texoma's charming little islands, it's back to the dock, which is filled with friendly boats owned by friendly people who love to party. You may be here longer than you think. In fact, for those who want another way to enjoy this area the Greer's also rent out a 1 bedroom condo (no smoking allowed) near the lake. Now covered by water is the site of Sophie Porter's famous home, Glen Eden. Sophie had four husbands and an extremely colorful life. Glen Eden was known all over Texas for the fabulous parties Sophie held, and her wine cellar was the finest. However, Sophie's big claim to fame was that she managed to lure Union soldiers down to the wine cellar, get them drunk, and then ride off to warn the Confederates that they were being pursued.

Over at **Grandpappy Point Marina and Restaurant** you'll find charming cottages for rent and outstanding food. Sailboats of every size dock here because Lake Texoma is a sailboat paradise.

And you don't want to miss **Fink, Texas**. Linda and Ron Ivey have bought the entire town of Fink, which consists of the Fink Motel, the Fink Deli, the Fink Convenience Store, and the Fink Gas Station—all in one building. The T-shirts are great, and just about everybody will want to know where Fink, Texas is. Incidentally, Fink is just immediately north of Pottsboro on FM 120.

You are just a few miles from **Denison**, where Dwight David Eisenhower was born in a modest frame home on October 14, 1890. Now the structure is a national shrine.

Stop by the Chamber of Commerce in Pottsboro and pick up brochures on all the events and attractions in this lovely part of Texas.

FAR FLUNG ADVENTURES

P.O. BOX 31
Terlingua 79852
915-371-2489
(Reservations: 800-359-4138)

Rates: $$ to $$$ (special rates available for groups)

Location: Terlingua is on the western edge of Big Bend National Park.

Amenities: Raft trips available from one to seven days. Spring and fall trips recommended. Far Flung will make your hotel/motel reservations. Floating Feasts (gourmet raft trips now available) with Francois Maeder, owner of San Antonio's Crumpet's Restaurant. Charter Music Trips with Steve Fromholz now available. "Saddles and Paddles" Trips with a day or two spent on horseback plus the Santa Elena Canyon float trip.

Restrictions: Reservations required for all raft trips. No pets.

Far Flung Adventures—even the name is romantic. Just hearing the name makes you anticipate a trip to little-known and unexplored places. I've been rafting down the Rio Grande with Far Flung Adventures several times and each trip was peaceful, yet exhilarating. It's all of the adventure and thrill you yearn for.

I'll never forget my first trip with Far Flung. When we arrived at Terlingua on our motorcycles we were already grubby and equipped with only the bare essentials for two days in the blistering sun and one night in a sleeping bag. Suddenly, a brand new Suburban pulled up and six women from Beaumont emerged looking like fashion plates from the Eddie Bauer catalog. You certainly wouldn't expect them to load and unload a raft and get those expensive clothes dirty. I felt like the world's biggest frump—even my new BMW motorcycle seemed frumpy. One lady was a Katherine Hepburn look-a-like, adorned with a floppy hat, dark glasses, cotton gloves, long pants, and a shirt. Only a tiny corner of her mouth was visible.

Finally, we all got organized and got in the river in Lajitas. Even though it was only Easter, that sun was hot. The trip was sort of dull at first, but then I realized the wonderful stillness that was all around us. Buzzards circled lazily overhead, an occasional stray donkey would bray his resentment at being disturbed during breakfast, and the whole scene was so placid it was almost unreal.

The Rio Grande isn't famous for its white water, so it's not a continual chills and spills trip. It's a release of all the stress and tension of life in the fast lane. Even the younger rafters were impressed by the calming effect of the river.

When we stopped for our lunch of cold cuts and chips, everyone was starved. You are expected to help carry the food and ice chests up to the picnic site and be generally helpful. Well, the Beaumont ladies joined in with vigor. We never saw Katherine Hepburn's face the entire trip, but she and the rest of the girls were virtual Amazons when it came to lifting and hauling. They never got dirty, but they certainly did more than their share of the work. Even at the end of the trip when we were all red, hot, sweaty, and grimy, they were starched, pressed, and clean. We found out later they had just finished two weeks of wilderness survival in Colorado, and this raft trip was their "treat" before returning to the real world.

Late in the afternoon we pulled up on a sand bar, and this time we really unloaded the rafts. Out came the tarps, sleeping bags, and boxes of gear. After we had the gear ashore, just about everyone headed for a dip in the river.

The guides did all the cooking, but we all did our share of arranging the gear. Of course, we were ravenous again, but what are raft trips for?

The guides were not only experts with paddles and oars, they knew how to turn out superb campfire fare. How about a steak cooked to perfection with hash browns, Texas toast, and salad? Talk about licking your platter clean—we were masters at the art. Then we sat around and chatted about the perfect day, the good food, where we were from, why we came on the trip, and how it was everything and more than we expected. Early that evening, very early, it was sleeping bag time with the sand for a mattress, the stars for night lights, and a few lonesome coyotes howling us to sleep.

Since we went to bed with the birds, we also got up with them. Our chef/guide was busy making coffee and a huge breakfast of bacon, eggs, and hash browns. We all trooped down to brush our teeth and "bathe" in the muddy Rio Grande. The toilet facilities were limited to wherever you took the roll of toilet paper. The way we attacked breakfast that morning, you would think it was the first, last, and only meal of the trip.

Then we packed up, loaded the rafts, and cast off. We floated calmly for a few hours, and then we banked the rafts. A gigantic wall of boulders blocked the river. We were about to enter the Rockslide area and Santa Elena Canyon. The guides climbed that impressive hunk of rock and sat, talked, pointed, and scratched their head for about an hour as we all wondered what the problem was. When the guides came down, we were given explicit instructions as to how to maneuver through the Rockslide area with our paddles and rafts. Mostly we just had to do whatever the guides ordered.

What a thrill! What fun! The Rockslide was definitely the

highlight of the trip. Those hard rubber rafts bounced off boulders as tall as Houston's skyscrapers, and we felt the hard spray of white water soaking us to the bone. It was absolutely glorious! Through those narrow channels we ricocheted with screams and yells of pure delight. This was what rafting was all about! It could go on forever!

Finally, we rode the channel to a still pool of water with the steep incredible walls of Santa Elena Canyon looming above and casting dark shadows over our small crafts. It would not be long now before we reached the quiet waters of our takeout point, bringing our adventure to an end. A wave of sadness fell over our raft.

It was a scruffy, bedraggled group (except for the Beaumont ladies) that rode the jaw-jolting miles back to Terlingua. All of us wanted to go to Lajitas and do it all over again. But, that's what Big Bend does to you—one trip, and you're hooked forever. A part of you always wants to come back.

Well, I went back to Big Bend, and I went back for Far Flung's same trip. It was just as wonderful, perhaps more so, the second time. All that was missing were the fashion plate ladies from Beaumont. I can't wait for the next trip, and the next, and the next.

An ideal getaway time would be the first week in November when Far Flung holds its **River Music** trek. About nine rafts float nineteen miles loaded with food, people, and gear while listening to the music bouncing off the walls of Santa Elena Canyon. You can count on musicians such as Steve Fromholz, Butch Hancock, and Jimmie Dale Gillmore to do a great deal of howling at the moon. What could be better than singing a Texas song with the Rio Grande for a backdrop?

Far Flung Adventures offers raft trips through all of Big Bend's canyons, lasting as long as 7 days. Or you can take a saddles and paddles trip, traveling by raft and horseback for 5 days. Trips are available for groups of sight- and mobility-impaired people. Far Flung also offers several other specialty options; Jim Bones runs a photo workshop, the Audubon Society leads a bird-watchers trip, and the Crumpets Gourmet Trip is a treat for any food lover. You'll probably want to try the white water of Arizona, New Mexico, Mexico, and Colorado. Far Flung offers these trips as well. Far Flung Adventures' motto is "Putting people . . . and rivers together," and they do a fantastic job of it.

HOTEL TURKEY WESTERN SWING HERITAGE TOUR

Hotel Turkey
P.O. Box 37
Turkey 79261
806-423-1151
800-657-7110

Hosts: Jane and Scott Johnson

Accommodations: Hotel Turkey 26 rooms, 15 baths Amarillo, Fifth Seasons Inn (From Amarillo, tour includes 3 days, 2 nights, but not all meals. From Dallas, tour includes 4 days, 3 nights, but not all meals. Call for dates and brochures.)

Rates: $$

Location: Turkey is about 125 miles northeast of Lubbock and southeast of Amarillo at the junction of SH 70 and SH 86.

Amenities: Surrey rides, restaurant, incredible West Texas ambiance.

Restrictions: Smoking in designated area only, no pets.

"Bob Wills is still the king."
Waylon Jennings

Waylon Jennings was absolutely right when he said, "Bob Wills did more for Texas and our kind of music than any other musician." The "King of Western Swing" and the originator of this unique swing style of music was born in Turkey and christened James Robert Wills in 1906. His dad called him "Jim Rob," but "Jim Rob" changed to Bob after a stint as the town barber. When Bob was in his early twenties, he left Turkey far behind. For 24 years Wills' "Ahhhh-ha" was as popular as his classic "San Antonio Rose."

The King died in 1975 after composing more than 500 songs, making scores of movies, and influencing western music more than any other artist. He was admitted to both the Country Music Hall of Fame as well as the National Cowboy Hall of Fame. Now, during the last weekend of every April, Turkey celebrates Bob Wills' Day. Bob Wills' backup band, the Texas Playboys, are still playing and they show up, helping to make this one of the best festivals in Texas. How can you resist "Spanish Two-Step," "Maiden's Prayer," "Faded Love," "Ida Red," and "Time Changes Everything?" Turkey also erected a monument to their favorite son, and it wins the Texas Tacky Award hands down. An 8-foot granite base is topped with a gigantic aluminum shaft with a double-sided fiddle, and, yes, it does rotate and play Bob Wills' songs. Ahhhh-ha!

Well, Jane and Scott Johnson want to share Turkey with the rest of the world, and they have arranged some terrific soirees into the mystique of West Texas. You can either be picked up by the tour bus in Amarillo or Dallas before you head out for the Lone Prairie. You'll have one night at Jane and Scott's historic Hotel Turkey, get a surrey ride pulled by the hotel's pet horse appropriately named Gobbler, take a tour of Turkey (it doesn't take long), get your picture taken by the Bob Wills Monument, visit the little Bob Wills Museum, listen to a fascinating cowboy poet, meet Thunder and Lightning (the potbellied pigs), and eat some of the best downhome cooking south of the Red River. What's for breakfast? Scott's "Turkey cakes," of course.

Hotel Turkey originally opened in 1927 and has never been closed, although it did fall on some very hard times. Scott is a native of Turkey, and when the hotel came up for sale, he gave up being a city boy to return home and become a hotelier. It wasn't easy getting the decrepit old building back in shape, particularly when big hardware stores are a long way off. But, the old Turkey Hotel is now better than ever. Decorated with Jane's eclectic collection of stuff and things, the result is total charm.

Also part of this Western Swing Tour is the **American Quarterhorse Museum** in Amarillo, the **Panhandle Plains Historical Museum** in Canyon, a **Cowboy Breakfast** at the Figure 3 Ranch, a drive through the rugged, scenic beauty of **Caprock Canyons State Park**, a visit to **Nance Ranch**, which is just outside of Canyon, where guests visit a working ranch and learn about cattle branding, sheep shearing, milking, and other ranch jobs. Then it's chow time so your tour includes a big steak at the legendary **Big Tex** restaurant. If you eat a 72-ounce steak in one hour, it's yours for free. And, what would a trip out to West Texas be without a shopping spree at Amarillo's big western wear store, **Boots & Jeans**! Here are the clothes the stars wear! During the summer months you will also attend the fabulous production of "Texas" in Palo Duro Canyon. If time allows, antique lovers will want to head for **Sixth Street**, originally old Route 66. Fascinating shops full of trash and treasures line both sides of Sixth Street.

So pardners, dust off your boots, pull on your jeans, put a crease in your Stetson, and head 'em up and roll 'em out for Turkey. The wild and wooly Panhandle Plains are waiting to show you how the West used to be.

TIMBER RIDGE TOURS
OF THE BIG THICKET

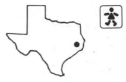

P.O. Box 115
Kountze 77625
409-246-3107

Hosts: James and Nelda Overstreet

Accommodations: Primitive camping or one modern cottage.

Tour times: April through September, Saturday and Sunday 1 P.M., 3 P.M., and 5 P.M.

Rates: $

Location: Take Highway 96 north of Beaumont. Take bypass around Silsbee until 4 miles north of Silsbee. Look for official National Park sign. Exit right and follow signs to Timber Ridge Tours.

Amenities: Picnic area, 12-passenger pontoon boat with full canopy and wheelchair accessibility.

Restrictions: No pets, must bring own picnic food, drinks, and supplies.

The Big Thicket has always enjoyed a mysterious aura. Early Spanish explorers avoided this massive area of impenetrable woods, as did early Anglo-American settlers who named it the Big Thicket as early as the 1820s. During the Civil War, many Big Thicket residents retreated into the dense underbrush to escape fighting in what they considered to be a rich man's war. But during the lumber boom, the Big Thicket, which once sprawled over 3.5 million acres, shrank to a mere 300,000 acres. Finally, in 1974 the National Park Service took over what little was left of this preserve to maintain the remnant of its complex biological diversity.

What is so extraordinary about the Big Thicket is not the

rarity or abundance of life forms, but the large number of species that coexist here. Major North American biological influences bump up against each other in the southeastern swamps, eastern forests, central plains, and southwestern deserts. Bogs sit near arid sandhills and eastern bluebirds nest near western roadrunners. Species of orchids grow next to cacti, and four of North America's five types of insect-eating plants live in the Big Thicket. Birds, reptiles, amphibious frogs and toads, shrubs and flowering plants from floodplain forests, hardwood forests, cypress sloughs, and savannahs all coexist in this rare ecological system.

To see the Big Thicket, let James and Nelda Overstreet give you a firsthand look into its wilderness, history, legends, and facts. James and Nelda have been approved by the Big Thicket National Preserve, Texas Parks and Wildlife, American Red Cross, and even the US Coast Guard, so you know they know about traveling in the Big Thicket. In fact, James' ancestors migrated here way back when Texas was barely known as Texas, and the family never left.

Before you board the pontoon boat, James and Nelda show off their collection of photographs of the flora and fauna from the Big Thicket so you'll know what you just might run into on your 90-minute cruise on the Nueces River. After boarding the boat, James gives a humorous, informative nature talk about the oddities of Mother Nature as seen in the Big Thicket. You're given a life jacket, but you don't really need one.

Then the cruise begins. At the old railroad bridge, James tells how Bonnie and Clyde rode this 1906 relic when they were hiding out in nearby Daisetta. It was the last turning trussel in southeast Texas, and it made it's last go-round in 1913. Then, James spins the tale of the Kaiser Burnout. Seems like a lot of Big Thicket "Jayhawkers" didn't intend to fight for the Confederacy at all, so they just disappeared from the face of the earth in the Big Thicket. Johnny Rebs didn't like that at all, so in an effort to capture these deserters, a massive fire was set to burn them out. It really didn't work—the Big Thicket was just too big—but it makes a good story.

After bouncing off some cypress knees up one of the many sloughs off the Nueces River, it's time for lunch. James beaches the pontoon on a large white sandbar, and a card table is set up, where you can spread out your lunch under the shade of a willow tree. Watch carefully or you might step on turtle eggs buried in the sand. Then, it's just about time to mosey on back to the dock and return from absolute quiet to the hurried pace at home.

But, if you yearn for even more of the Big Thicket experience, don't worry. James and Nelda offer other trips (from February to November) in conjunction with Customized Outdoor Adventures. You can set up your own fishing, boating, hiking, biking, riding, nature, and historical tour with special guides.

Also, while you are touring the Big Thicket area, see the **Rural Life Museum** on **Pelt Pond Farm** out of Kountze (409–287–3300) and the **Big Thicket Museum** in Saratoga (409–274–5000), plus the National Park Service has a plethora of nature programs for kids and adults of all ages. James and Nelda will be delighted to send you all of these brochures, or you can write the National Park Service, Big Thicket National Preserve, 3785 Milam, Beaumont 77701.

INDEX